A PRACTICAL APPROACH TO RSP

Second Edition

A PRACTICAL APPROACH TO RSP

A Handbook for the Resource Specialist Program

By

LESLIE ANN WILLIAMS, ED.D.
School Psychologist

and

LUCILE SWANSON ARNTZEN, M.S.
Resource Specialist

CHARLES C THOMAS • PUBLISHER
Springfield • Illinois • U.S.A.

Published and Distributed Throughout the World by

CHARLES C THOMAS • PUBLISHER
2600 South First Street
Springfield, Illinois 62794-9265

© *1994 by* CHARLES C THOMAS • PUBLISHER

ISBN 0-398-05908-X

Library of Congress Catalog Card Number: 94-525

With THOMAS BOOKS *careful attention is given to all details of manufacturing
and design. It is the Publisher's desire to present books that are satisfactory as to
their physical qualities and artistic possibilities and appropriate for their particular
use.* THOMAS BOOKS *will be true to those laws of quality that assure a good
name and good will.*

Printed in the United States of America
SC-R-3

.1782733   *1—20—95*

Library of Congress Cataloging-in-Publication Data

Williams, Leslie Ann.
    A practical approach to RSP : a handbook for the Resource
Specialist Program / by Leslie Ann Williams and Lucile Swanson
Arntzen. — 2nd ed.
        p.   cm.
    Includes bibliographical references (p.) and index.
    ISBN 0-398-05908-X
    1. Resource programs (Education)—Handbooks, manuals, etc.
I. Arntzen, Lucile Swanson.   II. Title.
LB1028.8.W55   1994
371.9—dc20   94-525
                                                       CIP

AUTHORS' NOTE

Looking back over our original manuscript, now over thirteen years old, we find that much of the information contained there remains basically the same. We find that our basic philosophies on public relations, assessment, discipline, scheduling, and instruction have remained the same as they were when we first encountered RSP. Legislative changes, innovations in materials and instructional techniques, however, have challenged us with this second edition.

PREFACE

Federal and state legislation have carefully outlined certain requirements for the Resource Specialist Program (RSP). Among these requirements are responsibilities to appraise parents of their rights; support and assist the staff with curriculum adjustments and modifications; assess and place students; provide in-service workshops for the staff in the various aspects of the Resource Specialist Program and varying handicapping conditions they may encounter; and write and implement an Individual Educational Plan (IEP) for each identified student. There is room within these requirements for adjustment and flexible interpretation, and the complexities of the Resource Specialist Program become obvious only as one initiates and implements the program. Flexibility and modification are vital aspects of the program. After working with the program for over thirteen years, the authors felt that the expertise gained as Resource Specialists could be shared with other and future Resource Specialists. It was felt that by sharing the ways these requirements had been met, other Resource Specialists might save needless time of trial, error and doubt. It is also felt that this book could provide a practical look at the Resource Specialist Program for future specialists in teacher training institutions or novices initiating their first program. Administrators might also be interested in information from the perspective of the Resource Specialist. The contents of this book are based primarily on firsthand experience. The ideas presented are not thought of by the authors as unique, but the authors felt that these ideas could be of benefit if put into written format for others.

The authors have chosen to present areas that they felt to be most important to the success of the Resource Specialist Program. These areas include public relations, the referral procedure, the assessment procedure and assessment measures, curriculum adjustment and modification in the content areas, discipline techniques, survival and study skills for RSP students, coping with the pressures of the Resource Specialist position,

vii

suggested planning schedules, the role of vocational and career education within RSP, case studies, and a materials and reference bibliography.

Since there is some flexibility within Public Law 94-142, much of the information presented in this book is based on the original California Master Plan (this state's interpretation of P.L. 94-142) as well as the IDEA Act which followed several years later. The basic tenet remains the same from state to state, and the difference may come merely in the implementation of the specific requirements.

These past years have proven to be a learning experience for the writers and it is hoped that the information presented may be of some help to others concerned with the education of these students with special needs.

We greatly appreciate the encouragement and assistance of our colleagues, students, families and friends during this project. Special thanks goes to Joan Williams and Janet McClanahan, our diligent and dedicated typists—they had the hard part.

L.A.W.
L.S.A.

INTRODUCTION

The concept of the Resource Specialist Program (referred to through-out the rest of this book as RSP) for mildly handicapped students was developed as a result of questions that arose about the education and social consequences of the segregated, self-contained classrooms and schools that, up to this time, served special needs students. It was felt that many students did not warrant restrictive, segregated instruction merely because they were in need of extra help. A great social need to be instructed alongside their peers was seen.

With these major concerns and the push toward educational equality for all handicapped individuals, parent support groups, teacher groups and lobbyists gathered together to support the passage of P.L. 94-142.

One of the changes that P.L. 94-142 brought about was a different delivery system for providing services to mildly handicapped students. One outcome of this was the RSP program where an identified student would come to receive specific instruction on a regularly scheduled basis while receiving the majority of his education in the regular classroom. The RSP classroom is only a small percentage of the student's program. An RSP student is pulled out of the regular classroom to be seen by the RSP teacher for up to 49% of his school day. RSP is considered an elective class just like art, music or industrial arts. The student receives math instruction in the regular classroom from the regular math teacher but may come to the RSP room for extra help with math.

RSP students are specifically those students who are able to function in the regular classroom successfully for the majority of the day and who require support in academic, language, math and/or perceptual areas. The program is not designed for students with severe handicaps or behavior disorders. The program serves students with minimal needs in the areas of language, reading, math and/or written language.

The Resource Specialist's duties seem to be overwhelming at times, but the major responsibilities may include the following:

1. the handling of referrals, and including assessments;
2. the writing and implementation of the Individualized Educational Program for each student in the program;
3. the coordination and presentation of in-service workshops for the staff;
4. the direct instruction of RSP students;
5. the coordination of program development between RSP and the regular classroom;
6. consultation with parents and staff.

There is still controversy over the advantages and disadvantages of the program. The writers feel that there are several advantages that deserve mention. The Resource Specialist has the opportunity to serve more students in her role as consultant to the regular classroom teacher. Students not identified or students who do not qualify for the program but do require some help can indirectly be helped by the Resource Specialist who is able to help the regular classroom teacher make adjustments in the curriculum for students other than identified RSP students, as well as the RSP students. The flexibility of the program allows the specialist to see students according to their needs. A student may only require assistance from the Resource Specialist a few times a week, and the specialist is able to accommodate that student's need and schedule within this program. Students may remain integrated in the regular classroom for the majority of the day and receive instruction with their peers, a vital aspect of the students' school careers. The stigma of labeling is removed by the RSP program and the self-contained classrooms remain the setting for those severely handicapped students who are not able to function successfully in the regular classroom for the majority of the day.

While there is still room for interpretation and change within the program, the authors feel that the program has seen success over the years. The success of the program requires the concerted cooperation of parents, students, teachers, administrators and Resource Specialists. The authors recognize the need for the Resource Specialists to be proficient in many areas beyond those required of the regular classroom teacher. This handbook addresses these areas.

It has also been recognized by the authors that there is controversy over the "de-sexing" of language in regard to education. The authors respect this concern of others but have chosen, for their own reasons, to address teachers throughout this book as *her* and students as *him*. This is not meant for any other reason on the part of the authors.

CONTENTS

A PRACTICAL APPROACH TO RSP

Chapter 1

PUBLIC RELATIONS

Resource Specialist competencies covered in Chapter 1: The Resource Specialist must demonstrate the ability to—
1. define the Resource Specialist Program including its goals and services;
2. present information to parents, teachers, and students without attaching value judgments;
3. explore problem areas, define the problem, and decide on a course of action;
4. use good interpersonal communication skills for reinforcement and reporting purposes;
5. maintain concise, legible records.

Public relations has played a most significant role in our own success as Resource Specialists. It has provided a very sound foundation on which to build an effective program. A good working relationship with both staff and administration can help get the program off to a good start and maintain success throughout the year.

The most important component of any good relationship is COMMUNICATION. This is especially true for the Resource Specialist as well as all special educators who must deal daily with frustrated staff members, busy administrators, angry parents and troubled students.

One of the roles that the Resource Specialist will have to play is that of consultant. Resource Specialists are unique in that they share their students with other teachers, yet must keep abreast of the student's progress in that other class. Therefore, it becomes very important for the specialist to devote time to consultation.

A good consultant in any field tries to help people find their own solutions and answers to problems and questions. The Resource Specialist, as a consultant, will help teachers, parents, and students find their own answers and make their own decisions. More than merely giving answers, the Resource Specialist will define the steps involved in the problem-solving and decision-making process regarding RSP students. The

Resource Specialist will supply the information by which decisions can be made and problems can be solved.

Acting as a consultant enables the Resource Specialist to extend assistance to students who are in need of extra help but are ineligible for the Resource Specialist Program. Consultation with staff or administrators may include the following:

1. discussion of educational and/or behavior problems of specific students,
2. presentation of supplementary materials for use with the regular curriculum,
3. presentation of alternative texts and materials for use in place of those used in a regular curriculum,
4. presentation of other curriculum adaptation skills and procedures,
5. follow-up on students no longer in the program,
6. observation of students who have been referred to the program,
7. exploration of ways to individualize the regular classroom curriculum,
8. sharing of professional information of benefit to the Resource Specialist, teacher and student.

Good communication and consultation skills involve not just imparting information but being a good listener as well. The Resource Specialist must be willing to listen to teachers, parents, and students and realize that at times they may need to vent their anger and frustration. This may be directed toward the Resource Specialist or the program but not necessarily mean that they are angry with one or the other. It is important not to take this personally. Parents, teachers, and students must, however, know that you are willing to listen to their concerns, and eventually you may be able to convince them to vent their anger and frustration in more constructive directions. Communication will be lost if your students, their parents, and your colleagues feel that they cannot come to you with their concerns. It is necessary for the Resource Specialist set aside a certain amount of time each day for the purpose of consultation, whether with parents, teachers, students or administrators.

IN-SERVICE PROGRAMS

There are four major populations that need to be reached when planning an in-service program — administrators, staff (teachers), parents and students. It is especially important to reach all four when you begin to implement the program because you will need the support of each group for a totally successful program. It is important to remember how each group fits into your plan and approach them accordingly. It is important to design your in-service workshop to suit the needs of the group with which you will be speaking.

If you are setting up a new RSP program you will probably want to contact the administrators first because you will want to have their support in everything you do. All administrators are extremely busy, so plan your in-service workshop carefully. Be brief, to the point, and clear in the presentation. The following points should be included in the in-service workshop for administrators:

1. definition of the Resource Specialist Program,
2. how the program will be implemented into the total school plan and schedule,
3. the responsibilities of each administrator under the new program,
4. exactly what type of support will be needed from them,
5. what services they and the other teachers can expect from the RSP teacher,
6. a brief explanation of the referral procedure and eligibility criteria,
7. a question-and-answer period so concerns may be voiced.

It is hoped that you will leave the in-service workshop with the support of the administrators and their willingness to participate in in-service programs for the rest of the staff. One meeting may not be enough, and it is sometimes a good idea to cover the most important aspects of the program first and then have follow-up meetings to go into more detail. These may be scheduled at the in-service workshop or left to later scheduling. You will want to leave your administrators with brief guide-lines of the program.

When planning an in-service program for the teachers it should be done with the knowledge and support of the administration. This part of the in-service plan may be the most important because ultimately the success of the program will depend on how well the regular classroom teachers accept the new program. A teacher in-service program should be ongoing, providing a means for continual growth for both Resource Specialist and regular classroom teacher. You will want to make yourself available to your staff as a whole and also on an individual basis.

In-service programs for staff members can be done in many different ways. Knowing the staff can of course enable you to choose the best approach. If you are a new Resource Specialist (or new to your school) you will definitely want to consult your administrator, school psychologist or counselor when planning the in-service program. Initially, you will need to conduct a general in-service workshop to introduce the program. Ideally, this should be done before the implementation of the new program, either the first week of school, the week before the students return from summer vacation, or the week or term before the program is initiated. Topics that will need to be covered in the initial in-service workshop include the following:

1. definition of the Resource Specialist Program,
2. the purpose of the program,
3. the way the program will be set up,
4. the role and responsibility of the Resource Specialist; how the RSP teacher can and will help the regular classroom teacher,
5. the role and responsibilities of the regular classroom teacher; stressing the idea of teamwork,
6. the referral procedure,
7. the importance of confidentiality of all information on students in the program,
8. brief instruction in curriculum adaptations; a more detailed in-service workshop will probably be required at a later date.

It is important not to flood the teachers with too much information. Remember that this is a very new and different program and some people may not take to this change with much enthusiasm. At this first in-service workshop you may want to schedule later meetings; include the teachers in this scheduling. If they are included and are aware that this is something for their benefit, they will be more willing to participate. Future in-service workshops could be done with small groups during conference periods or with the entire staff. It could be done topically; the program could be broken down and a brief in-service workshop offered on each aspect. The staff should be included in planning the type of future in-service workshop they prefer.

One way to involve the staff in future in-service programs is through a needs assessment and organizing small workshops based on the staff's responses. This will ensure that relevant topics will be covered. Be sure to tell the staff that the purpose of the questionnaire is to prepare future in-service programs for them. Once they know the reason behind the questionnaire, the response will probably be greater. One point to remember when passing out any kind of communication that requires a response is to put a return date on it, follow up with a note or reminder a couple of days before the return date, and do not give too long a time in which to return it. You will know how much time to allow as you become more acquainted with your staff; twenty-four hours may not be enough for some, and a week may be too much. Just give a reasonable amount of time to respond and let them know the return date. A piece of candy goes a long way in getting things returned even from adults!

However you plan the in-service, it is always necessary to design it to suit the needs and personality of your staff.

Even though you have spent hours planning your in-service program, sending out questionnaires and are sure you have covered all topics the teachers expressed interest in, this does not insure a successful in-service program. Teachers do not always come to an in-service workshop with a positive attitude no matter what the topic is! It is vital that you catch their interest within the first few minutes and convince them that you have something of interest to them. Include your staff; do not stand in front of them and lecture for hours. In addition to including the staff in the planning of the in-service program (through the needs assessment), you will need to include them in carrying out the in-service workshop as well. There are several ways to include your staff.

Role playing and cooperative learning activities are methods often used by teachers to gain the participation of their students. It can also be an excellent way to gain teacher interest and participation at an in-service workshop. Many aspects of the Resource Specialist Program can be portrayed through role playing—the referral procedure, discipline techniques, methods of curriculum adjustment, attitudes toward mainstreaming and other concepts.

Another way to capture the interest of the staff at an in-service workshop is through the use of handouts. Briefly highlighting important aspects of the program in writing will give the teachers something tangible for future reference. The following are some things you may want to include in your handouts:

1. the steps involved in referring a student for assessment,
2. a few signs or behaviors which could indicate that a student may have some special needs,
3. possible behavior handling tips; many negative behaviors indicate something more than just the child's desire for attention,

4. materials that may be of interest and use to them (this may be broken down by subject area for quick reference).

In using handouts, be sure that you do not pass them out before you present the material yourself. If you pass out the handouts first, you may lose your entire audience.

Recently, videos, films, and filmstrips have been made on the issue of mainstreaming and its effect on the entire school. These may be of use with some staffs. Visual material is usually a good way to capture the interest of most audiences. In the last chapter of this book, a bibliography will include some visual materials that you may wish to include in your in-service program.

Parents are often forgotten when planning an in-service program. The in-service program for parents will take quite a different perspective from that for teachers and administrators. Parents are interested in different things and may be even more resistant to change than some teachers. Parents have definite fears that are not shared by teachers. Because of these fears, they may prefer a more segregated setting as in the old self-contained classroom. Parents may fear that their child will not get enough help in this new program and that he will get lost in the "mainstream." They may be afraid of the reaction of nonhandicapped children to their child. Sometimes children can be cruel and parents may not want their child exposed to such threats. Whatever the arguments against the program or fears about it, the goals of the Resource Specialist Program should be carefully described. Once parents understand the benefits of the program they will be less reluctant to change. They must be reassured that their child will be getting the help of the regular classroom teacher now as well as the help of the Resource Specialist. They must be assured that this experience will help their child prepare for adulthood. They must understand that their help is needed in planning an effective program for their child and that teamwork and cooperation are vital for their child's success. Parents will also want to know what you are doing to help their child and what they can do at home to reinforce that. They will want to know about the assessment tools you will be using to determine their child's present levels of functioning. They will want to know what materials you are using with their child. You may even be able to suggest some materials that they can use at home with their child.

The most important thing to stress to parents is that you and the regular classroom teachers are all working with them to help their child. It is also essential to stress the importance of developing any positive aspects and qualities of the child. Concentrate on the positive while strengthening the less positive areas. It is easy for people to get caught up in negatives, devoting all their energy to bringing about positive changes, and forget the positive aspects that already exist. Positive reinforcement is vital to everyone's success, especially the child with special needs. Make sure that parents leave the in-service workshop with a positive attitude toward the program. Their attitudes can easily be transferred to their children, so it is important that you leave them with good feelings about the program and their child.

In-service workshops for the parents may not need to be as frequent as that for the teachers. Special Education teachers seem to hold frequent parent conferences throughout the year and the same will be true for the Resource Specialist. Whenever you do an in-service workshop you will need the support of your administration. Your principal may have information to share; the school counselor, psychologist, or nurse may also have information to share, so you will not want to overlook any of these people when planning an in-service workshop.

The group that is almost always forgotten when planning an in-service program is students. Special educators have always felt that it is important to have the cooperation of administrators, teachers, and parents, but they often overlook the importance of student cooperation. A student's self-image is determined by many factors, one of them being how he is perceived by his peers. If a child is put down, teased, or ridiculed by his classmates, he may feel a sense of personal failure. This may of course affect his schoolwork. Special educators have been dealing with the stigma of Special Education and labeling and its effects on students for years. Now, with the implementation of mainstreaming and inclusion, students with the more severe physical and mental disabilities will be mainstreamed or integrated into the regular school classroom. For many of them this will be their first consistent interaction with nonhandicapped students. They will ultimately be perceived as different by their classmates. It is up to us as Resource Specialists to work with these students and prepare them to be able to deal with any problem they may encounter as a result of mainstreaming. It is also up to us to reach out to the nonhandicapped students and help prepare them to deal with handicapped students. Nonhandicapped students are probably not aware that they can have a profound impact on another student's life; if not channeled properly, that impact can be disastrous. It is hoped that this will go beyond the school setting for both handicapped and nonhandicapped students and prepare them for future life situations.

COMMUNICATION AFTER THE WORKSHOP

A very defined and systematic approach will insure ongoing and open communication among staff members, Resource Specialist, parents and students. It is essential that the Resource Specialist develop a system of divulging, receiving, and recording information that is concise and legible.

All information about a student in the Resource Specialist Program (or any student who may have been referred and did not qualify) is strictly confidential, and the Resource Specialist should use discretion in sharing pertinent information with teachers and other staff members involved with the student. It is required by Special Education regulations that a log be kept naming all persons who review the student's confidential file. Each district will have its own system for recording such information.

The Resource Specialist will need to be aware of what information to share with specific teachers. For example, a history teacher should be aware of the student's reading ability but would not necessarily need to know about the student's math ability. If a student cannot read a ruler, he may have trouble in wood shop. His shop teacher should be aware of this so that he could, with the Resource Specialist, develop a plan to help the student learn how to read a ruler. The shop teacher needs to be informed of this long before that project is due; last-minute excuses usually do not go over well with most teachers. It is the responsibility of the Resource Specialist to share this information with the shop teacher.

Most regular classroom teachers have not had the training (that Special Education teachers have had) to interpret formal assessment scores. Therefore, a score of 7 on the Digit Span subtest on the Wechsler Intelligence Test for Children-Revised may be meaningless to the regular classroom teacher. The score will take on meaning, however, when the Resource Specialist or the School Psychologist explain that the student may have difficulty with short-term auditory memory. Translated, this means that the student may have difficulty understanding and retaining a series of oral directions. You may suggest to the teacher that the student be given directions one at a time or in written form as well as in oral form. Be sure to ask the teacher for suggestions; do not dictate how the teacher should do his job. Your approach might be, "How can we help the student remember his assignments and directions better?" Come up with solutions together. That is the purpose of the Resource Specialist, and remember your role as consultant.

All information that the Resource Specialist receives or gives out will need to be recorded. It is imperative to document all phone calls with parents and conferences with teachers and any other involved individuals. Remember that your records must be available at all times to parents.

In addition, the Resource Specialist needs to develop consistent communication policies with staff members. Frequent communication is necessary for an effective program. Communication can be adapted to suit the schedule of each staff. The following are just a few suggestions as to how communication can be consistently maintained:

1. written weekly progress reports from each teacher who has an RSP student,
2. the Resource Specialist may attend departmental meetings on a regular basis,
3. individual conferences may be scheduled with teachers on their conference periods,
4. informal conferences during lunch,
5. weekly written progress reports to parents.

Accurate recording takes up much of the Resource Specialist's valuable time, but it can be kept to a minimum if time is set aside each day for the required paperwork.

Remember that the rapport you develop with your staff and administration and parents, along with the system of communication you maintain, will determine the success of the Resource Specialist Program in your school. These provide the foundation on which you will build your program. It is important to remember also that the Resource Specialist is not one who can avoid that certain teacher whose ideas and opinions are different or offensive. The Resource Specialist must be able and willing to deal with all staff members; they may not have to like each other, but they have to be able to work together and not (as my principal once told me) wear their feelings on their shirt-sleeves. We are all human, we all have feelings, and this is indeed a very difficult position to take. However, we are also intelligent, educated adults, capable of assuming the responsibility necessary to carry out this position. With this in mind, the following are a few important highlights of this chapter that you may want to remember:

1. Good rapport and open communication are key factors in a successful Resource Specialist Program.
2. One role of the Resource Specialist is as a consultant whose purpose is to help teachers and parents examine problems and determine their own ways of solving them, perhaps finding alternate approaches as well.
3. In-service programming for administrators, teachers, parents, and students is a complex, integral part of the Resource Specialist Program.
4. The Resource Specialist Program requires teamwork to succeed; the cooperation of the Resource Specialist, administration, staff, parents, and student is vital to the program.
5. The Resource Specialist is required to develop a consistent and legible system of receiving, divulging, and recording information about all students in the program. All of this information must be kept strictly confidential.
6. Frequent communication and documentation of all correspondence should be practiced by the Resource Specialist.

Chapter 2

THE REFERRAL PROCEDURE

Resource Specialist competencies covered in Chapter 2: The Resource Specialist must demonstrate the ability to—
1. prepare for, schedule and preside over meetings;
2. select appropriate data related to an individual student to present at meetings;
3. complete forms necessary in the referral procedure;
4. interpret assessment data and write an IEP based on those data.

The referral procedure outlined by P.L. 94-142 may appear to be quite complex. It is therefore necessary to follow prescribed guidelines carefully. The specific steps may vary somewhat from district to district, consortium to consortium, state to state, but, basically, the format remains the same.

The first step is the referral itself. Any teacher, administrator, counselor, or parent may refer a student for review. The person making the referral must submit in writing the following:

1. date of referral;
2. an objective description of the student's behavior that raised question or concern;
3. a record of the student's academic progress in the referring teacher's class. In case of a referral from someone other than a teacher, specific academic problems or weaknesses may be substituted;
4. specific steps the referring person has taken to help the student or to modify the inappropriate behavior, i.e. interventions (without concrete examples the referral may not be submitted);
5. documentation that this concern has already been discussed with the parents.

The referral is submitted to the chairperson of the IEP team, usually the principal or his designee. Upon receipt of the referral, the student's other teachers may be requested to complete a progress report including academic and behavioral performance, attendance, attitude, relationship with peers and any additional relevant comments. The student's cumulative file may also be reviewed for information about possible previous problems.

The principal or his designee schedules a meeting to discuss the information received and options available. Some of these options may include academic assessment by the Resource Specialist and/or a designated Instructional Services representative (Speech Pathologist, hearing or vision specialist, adaptive P.E., etc.), schedule adjustment, assignment modification, performance monitoring, or the referral may even be dismissed. This group may be called Student Study Team, Child Study, Pupil Personnel Review, or Consultation Committee, and may consist of the following members:

1. principal or designee
2. school counselor
3. school psychologist
4. school nurse
5. Resource Specialist
6. referring teacher
7. Speech Pathologist
8. parent, child advocate, Social Services worker or student

This group includes but is not limited to the members of the IEP team.

The members of the IEP team consist of at least the principal, Resource Specialist and parent. These persons are required to attend the review meeting. It is important not to confuse a review meeting with an IEP. Before any action is taken in a student's behalf, a Child Study, Pupil Personnel Review, or Consultation Committee meets. This cannot be done without parental consent.

If the review committee decides that academic assessment would be beneficial, written permission is obtained by the parents at that time. The Resource Specialist then has a designated number of school days from the date of consent to complete the assessment.

The IEPT is required to meet upon completion of the assessment results and make recommendations for the student. Recommendations may include the following:

1. enrollment in the Resource Specialist Program,
2. Designated Instructional Services, i.e. Speech Therapy, Adaptive P.E., etc.,
3. home or hospital teaching,

4. remain in regular program with schedule or assignment adjustment,
5. monitor for future review.

If the assessment indicates that the student qualifies for placement in the Resource Specialist Program, the Resource Specialist, along with the parent, prepares the IEP. The IEP is a formal written statement of the student's level of functioning in the areas of academic, social/emotional, sensory/motor, self-help, communication and vocational skills. The IEP includes educational goals and short-term instructional objectives suited to the student's individual needs. Included also are methods of implementing objectives and measuring growth, a date for review, and the names of persons responsible for implementation.

Public Law 94-142 establishes the criteria for placement in the Resource Specialist Program. Each district or consortium may interpret these guidelines and establish specific criteria for placement in RSP within that district. Students shall be eligible for placement in RSP by the IEP team or IEPT when they have met the established criteria, provided that appropriate modifications have been made to meet their needs within the regular classroom and have been found unsuccessful. There are many important factors to consider for placement in RSP in addition to the assessment data. The following are other factors to be considered:

1. reports from the regular classroom teacher,
2. a review of school records,
3. direct observation of the student in the regular classroom,
4. parent interviews and their concerns.

Sufficient information should be obtained to compile a comprehensive educational plan that will be successful for the student. That information is to be included in the Psychoeducational Assessment report written by the school psychologist.

The assessment results are still the most pertinent information to be considered when placing a student in RSP. All areas are to be measured by standardized tests administered by specialists trained in test administration and interpretation.

A student may not be placed in the Resource Specialist Program if he falls in one or more of these categories:

1. has a history of slow but steady progress and is functioning within the instructional range of the classroom and/or his cognitive potential;

2. achievement lag is due primarily to unfamiliarity with the English language or cultural differences;
3. exhibits disruptive behavior in the classroom but is achieving at grade level academically.

The steps involved in the referral procedure have been summarized in Table I. Table II illustrates a time line of the steps involved in the referral procedure.

Table I

REFERRAL PROCEDURE

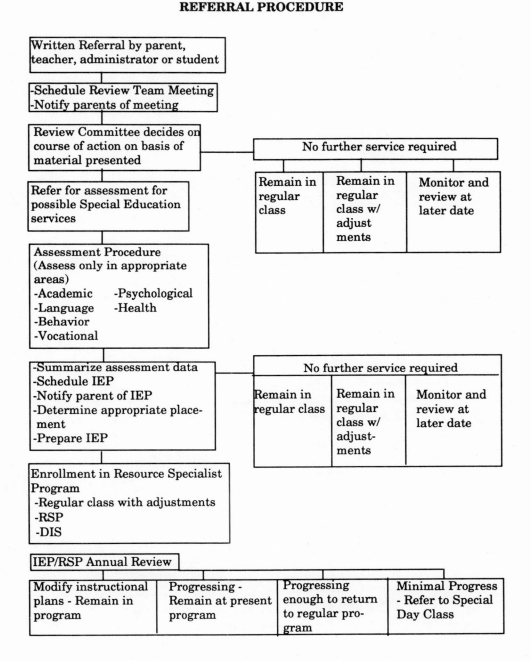

Table II

REFERRAL TIME LINE

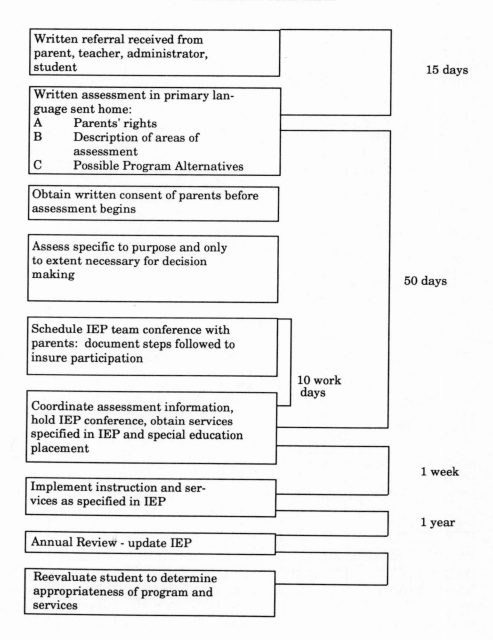

Written referral received from parent, teacher, administrator, student	15 days
Written assessment in primary language sent home: A Parents' rights B Description of areas of assessment C Possible Program Alternatives	
Obtain written consent of parents before assessment begins	
Assess specific to purpose and only to extent necessary for decision making	50 days
Schedule IEP team conference with parents: document steps followed to insure participation	10 work days
Coordinate assessment information, hold IEP conference, obtain services specified in IEP and special education placement	
Implement instruction and services as specified in IEP	1 week
Annual Review - update IEP	1 year
Reevaluate student to determine appropriateness of program and services	

Chapter 3

ASSESSMENT

Resource Specialist competencies covered in Chapter 3: The Resource
Specialist must demonstrate the ability to—
1. administer and score formal and informal type tests;
2. interpret assessment information and identify present levels of
   functioning;
3. use test results, along with observations and work samples, to
   prescribe the student's instructional program;
4. develop goals and short-term instructional objectives.

A very critical component of the Resource Specialist Program is the
assessment procedure. The student's academic future lies in the
interpretation of the assessment data. Because there is no fixed battery of
assessment tools mandated by P.L. 94-142, you will find that different
districts and consortiums use various assessment tools. Whichever measures are used, the purpose remains the same—to determine the strengths
and weaknesses of the student and to prescribe a plan to enable him to
experience success in school.

Prior to the actual testing, the parents must be notified that the testing
will take place. The parents are to be informed of the assessment tools to
be administered and the purpose of each. The parent must give written
permission, and the examiner then has *fifty* (50) days in which to complete the assessment.

It has been found helpful to meet with the student prior to the actual
testing. If possible, show the student where the testing will take place. It
has been found most beneficial to explain to the student that you will be
working with him on some different activities, some easy and others
maybe more challenging. This approach seems to be less threatening
than using the word "testing". Explain to him about how long each
session will be and when he will be seen by you. Try to explain to the
student why this is being done and that the results may help him be
successful in school. Reassure him that he will not be penalized for any
time missed from his classroom. It has often helped older students if

19

they can see the actual test itself. It is most important to put the student at ease before beginning the testing. Good rapport is critical, since most test results are hopefully assumed to be the student's optimal performance. Be sure to give the student a chance to ask any questions he might have about the testing procedure.

In addition to making the student as comfortable as possible about the testing, it is important that the examiner also be comfortable. The best way to achieve this is to be familiar with and qualified to administer the tests that are to be given. Make sure all of the required materials are available. Put other things aside and concentrate on the testing itself. The examiner's attitude will reflect in the student's attitude and performance.

If, during the testing, the student becomes overly frustrated or upset, it might be wise to discontinue testing until the student is more relaxed. Careful observance by the examiner will decide this. Also, remember that students tire easily in a testing situation. For young children, no more than twenty to thirty minutes should be spent testing at any one time. For older students the time may be increased. Testing for any student should be limited to forty-five to sixty minutes per session.

The remainder of the chapter has been devoted to a brief, annotated index of assessment tools that may be used in assessing for the Resource Specialist Program.

Tests of Academic Achievement

Brigance Diagnostic Inventories is a criterion-referenced test which assesses preacademic, academic, and vocational skills and assists in the definition of instructional goals and objectives. The test booklet (protocol) serves as an excellent log that can follow a student through school and record his progress in all areas covering skills from birth through grade twelve.

Kaufman Test of Educational Achievement (K-TEA) is an untimed, standardized test which assesses academic achievement in the comprehension and application of basic skills. The test correlates well with the school curriculum and is appropriate for students from ages six through eighteen.

Key Math Diagnostic Arithmetic Test is a standardized test which assesses arithmetic skills in the areas of facts, operations, concepts and application. Test score may provide sufficient information to determine eligibility, however, it may not be sufficient to develop specific programming objectives. Appropriate for use with students from grade one through grade six.

Peabody Individual Achievement Test—Revised is a standardized screening tool which assesses academic achievement and general information using a multiple-choice format. Interpretation of scores should be taken with caution because of the multiple-choice format and the assessor may need to supplement another test to assist in diagnostic planning. The test is appropriate for students from kindergarten through grade twelve.

Wechsler Individual Achievement Test (WIAT) is a diagnostic test of academic achievement which was developed to correlate with the Wechsler Intelligence scales. The *WIAT* is useful as a diagnostic tool, providing information helpful in implementing specific goals and objectives for students from kindergarten through grade twelve.

Wide Range Achievement Test—Revised (WRAT-R) is a screening tool which assesses general levels of functioning in basic spelling, arithmetic and word recognition. The *WRAT-R* should be administered only for screening purposes to students of all ages.

Woodcock-Johnson Psycho-Educational Battery—Revised is a comprehensive battery which assesses cognitive ability, academic achievement, aptitude and interests. The test is appropriate for ages three through adult. The administration, scoring, and interpretation of the test is difficult and proper instruction is critical.

Tests of Reading Ability

While the use of reading inventories may have decreased since the adoption of a whole language approach to reading, their value is still highly regarded in the diagnosis of specific reading disabilities and development of remedial programs.

Botel Reading Inventory assesses word recognition and reading comprehension skills through grade nine.

New Sucher-Allred Placement Inventory assesses word recognition and reading comprehension at the independent, instructional, and frustrational levels from a primer through ninth grade reading level.

Silveroli Classroom Reading Inventory screens students (and adults) in word recognition and reading comprehension but should be supplemented with other test data for specific program planning.

Spache Diagnostic Reading Scales assesses word recognition, reading comprehension, and phonics skills at the independent, instructional and frustration levels.

The examiner should keep in mind that performance on reading inventories can be directly related to the type of reading instruction the student has been receiving. Eligibility cannot be determined based on this type of assessment alone, but must be supplemented with other standardized processing and achievement data.

Tests of Cognitive Potential

Tests of cognitive ability are administered only by the school psychologist. These tests provide information about a student's potential and are necessary in determining eligibility and identification of processing disorders.

Kaufman Assessment Battery for Children (K-ABC) assesses two manners of processing information—sequential (serial ordered) and simultaneous (wholistical, integrated). The ability to process information and apply it to problem-solving situations yields achievement scores in arithmetic, reading decoding and reading comprehension. The K-ABC is used with English- and non-English-speaking children from ages three to twelve.

Stanford-Binet Intelligence Test—Fourth Edition assesses verbal comprehension, nonverbal reasoning (visualization, and memory in children and adults).

Wechsler Scales

Wechsler Preschool and Primary Scale of Intelligence (WPPSI) assesses verbal and nonverbal ability of young children from ages four through six years six months.

Wechsler Intelligence Scale for Children — Third Edition (WISC-III) assesses verbal (memory, conceptualization, vocabulary, reasoning, expression) and nonverbal (visual memory, visual sequencing, perceptual organization) ability in children ages six through sixteen.

Wechsler Adult Intelligence Scale—Revised (WAIS-R) assesses the same abilities as the *WISC-III* in individuals over the age of sixteen.

It is important for me at this point to digress from an overall description of tests in general and discuss the Wechsler scales in more detail. Since the first writing of this book I have completed extensive training as a school psychologist. It was during my training of the interpretation of the Wechsler scales that I realized how important this information would have been to me as an RSP teacher. During my years as a special education teacher, I never had the school psychologist explain these test scores to me. They remained a mystery and questions never seemed to be welcomed. I did not know whether I should be depressed or elated over a 7 on the Digit Span subtest and how critical the Comprehension and Picture Arrangement subtest scores could be in the social emotional development of the student. When I became a school psychologist, I vowed to do everything I could so that the special education and regular classroom teachers I would be working with had some knowledge of what these scores meant to them in their role as the teacher of each student.

Scoring, interpreting, and analyzing Wechsler scores is a very complex process and training is necessary and mandated for it. These scores are only one piece in the puzzle and must be compared to all other test data and information on the student in order to obtain a correct evaluation. Putting this puzzle together is the task of the school psychologist. The task of finding each student's own mean, or average, on each of the verbal and performance scales is the function of the school psychologist as well. But, it is possible for the special education and regular classroom teacher to become acquainted with each subtest, what it measures and how it relates to the student's performance in the classroom.

The interpretation of the WISC–III and the WAIS–R is basically the same in regard to the context of the age of the individual being assessed. For purposes of this discussion I will refer to the WISC–III (Wechsler Intelligence Scales for Children—Third Edition) which is appropriate for students from ages six through sixteen.

The WISC–III is divided into two major scales—verbal and performance or non-verbal. The verbal subtests require verbal responses while the performance subtests require manipulative responses. Language comprehension, however, does play an integral part in the performance component as the child needs to be able to understand oral directions as well as understand the modeling of the examiner.

The verbal subtests are as follows:

Information: This test is a measure of long-term auditory memory. The child is asked to recall items he has picked up at home and at school, but may not use on a daily basis. Low scores may indicate difficulty retaining information over a long period of time. For older students this can be critical because many content area courses cover units that may last several weeks. The use of a simple tape recorder on a daily basis to record a brief summary of information presented in class that day, and replayed periodically to review information, can be a tremendous help in retaining information. Students should be encouraged to practice this if they have a deficit in this area.

Similarities: This test is a measure of conceptual ability as well as logical and abstract thinking. It correlates highly with the overall verbal IQ score. Low scores may indicate difficulty generalizing concepts from information presented. Any instruction and learning that can be done in a multi-sensory fashion may enhance a student's ability in this area.

Arithmetic: This test is a measure of numerical reasoning without the aid of paper and pencil. This test also looks at concentration and is one of the critical subtests in evaluating Attention Deficit Disorder. Manipulatives and graphic illustrations may assist in this area.

Vocabulary: This test is a measure of receptive vocabulary, experiential background and verbal ability. It is important to determine whether low scores in this area are due to experience or true verbal deficiencies.

Comprehension: This test is a measure of common sense and social judgment. Low scores may suggest difficulty analyzing situations and problem solving. Role playing and everyday classroom and dinner table conversation about "What could you do if . . . " may enhance this area. Students with low scores in this area are often found to be those students that are frequently involved in disciplinary actions at home and at school. They appear to be devious or naughty and the real problem lies in their inability to problem solve and determine consequences of actions.

Digit Span: This test is a measure of short-term auditory recall. Low scores may indicate difficulty following directions, learning sequential data, and generally following along during activities. This is another test looked at in determining Attention Deficit Disorder, as it measures ability to pay attention and respond to immediate auditory stimulation. Mnemonics and multisensory activities are widely used to enhance this area.

The Performance subtests are as follows:

Picture Completion: This test is a measure of long-term visual memory for details. Low scores may result in poor spelling and math computation, and difficulty with information presented in a visual format. Auditory accompaniment may enhance retention of information presented visually.

Picture Arrangement: This test is a measure of common sense and social judgment and the ability to determine sequences of events and predict outcomes in social situations. Low scores may suggest difficulty planning and organizing one's daily activities. It may also result in difficulty with interpersonal relationships. This test is usually coupled with the Comprehension subtest in gaining information to substantiate any social problems a student may be having.

Block Design: This test is a measure of perceptual organization and correlates highly to the overall performance IQ. Low scores may result in poor organization and may require organizational aids for success.

Object Assembly: This test is a measure of perceptual organization as well that draws on an individual's past experiences and does not rely on a model from which to work. Low scores on this test, coupled with higher scores on the Block Design test, may indicate that working from a model is beneficial for the student's success. A reverse of that would suggest that the student does better working from his own imagination than from a model.

Coding: This test is a measure of short-term visual memory and visual-motor integration. It is the third critical subtest when determining an Attention Deficit Disorder. Low scores may suggest reduced concentration or actual visual-motor deficits. It is critical to compare this test score with other visual motor test data that has been obtained in order to draw an appropriate conclusion about the student's true ability.

Symbol Search: This test is a measure of visual discrimination and processing speed. Low scores may result in slow or reduced performance on written assignments.

Mazes: This test is a measure of motor planning and visual motor integration. Low scores may indicate difficulty with gross and fine motor planning and paper/pencil tasks.

This information about the Wechsler scales is clearly not sufficient to allow you to begin to analyze and interpret test scores. My purpose was to increase your awareness of what the test measures and how it relates to classroom performance. An excellent resource for specific, grade-by-grade remedial activities that correspond with each subtest is available from the publisher.

Tests of Visual Perception

> *Beery Developmental Test of Visual-Motor Integration (VMI)* screens visual-motor integration and a student's ability to copy geometric shapes and designs. The developmental age on this test alone cannot be taken to determine visual processing ability.
>
> *Bender Gestalt Test of Visual Motor Perception* is a commonly used test along with the *VMI* in determining specific visual-motor deficits in young children.
>
> *Motor-Free Visual Perception Test (MVPT)* assesses overall visual perceptual processing ability without motor accompaniment.

Great care must be taken when scoring each test. The manual should be referred to and used in interpretation. Upon completion of the testing, the parents are brought in to review the test results with the examiner at an IEPT meeting. Older students may also participate in the discussion of the test results. It is wise to check with the parents before the student is brought in. Test results showing great deficiencies may not want to be discussed with the student until after the parents have been consulted. A student may be told that he did very well remembering sounds he heard or letters he saw but may need some help remembering several directions at one time. He may be informed that he did very well on the whole number operations problems but may need some help understanding the steps involved in multiplying and dividing fractions. Always try to accent those areas in which the student did well. Do not present his deficiencies as something he cannot do. Instead, assure him that with a little extra help he will soon be able to multiply or divide fractions or perform other skills he has not yet mastered. Being honest with the parents and student as well will aid the remediation process. Everyone involved will have a clear understanding of just what needs to be worked on. Likewise, when a test indicates that the student is not in need of RSP services, it is important to communicate this to the student and parents. It should be stressed that the student needs to work very hard as he does have the ability and is not using that ability to the fullest extent.

The results of the assessment are filed in the student's cumulative file. A copy of the results may be given to the parents upon request, and a copy is sent to the Special Education coordinator. If the student qualifies for the RSP program, the Resource Specialist also retains a copy of the test results for her records. It is good practice to meet with the student's other classroom teachers to review briefly the student's test results. While not all teachers may understand what a score of 7 on the Digit Span subtest of the *WISC–III* means for the student in their classroom, they will understand when it is explained that the student has difficulty remembering what he hears in sequence. It could be suggested that the student not be given only oral directions. He will better retain directions if he can see them in writing as well as hear them. Most teachers appreciate this type of information and are more than willing to do all they can to help the student in their class. For purposes of confidentiality, regular classroom teachers should not be given copies of the test results, but it should be made known to them that the information is available to them in the student's cumulative file.

If the assessment data indicate that the RSP program would benefit the student, the IEP committee meets to write the IEP. The IEP is a written plan for each student with an identified need. The IEP must include present levels of academic and behavioral performance, long-range goals, short-term instructional objectives, Designated Educational Services, if necessary, evaluation procedure, time line, and persons responsible for implementing the IEP.

It is wise to keep in mind that the assessment procedure is a key component in the Resource Specialist Program. Everything that will be done for the student is determined by the assessment data. It is therefore critical to avoid any shortcuts in the assessment procedure and not to overlook any of the resulting data. To insure a positive experience for the student and comprehensive results for you, you may want to review and remember these points:

1. Parent permission is required for testing.
2. Discuss the tests to be used with parents and allow them to ask questions.
3. Meet with the student before you begin testing to ease his fears about the test; allow him to ask questions.
4. Administer the tests in a quiet, well-lighted environment that is conducive to optimal results; distractions should be avoided if possible.
5. Try to establish a good rapport with the student, since test results are usually assumed to be a student's optimal performance.
6. Encourage the student to do his best; praise should be given generously.

7. Record your answers in a way that the student cannot see what you are writing and become distracted.

8. Explain to the student that you cannot tell him how he did on each question but will be glad to go over the results of the total test when it has been scored.

9. Unless there is a penalty for guessing, students should always be encouraged to guess.

10. Discontinue testing if the student appears to be extremely frustrated or tired.

11. Be sure to write down any comments about the student's behavior during the test; this can be as helpful as the test results.

12. Make sure you have familiarized yourself with the test before beginning.

13. Make sure you have a positive attitude toward the test.

14. Prepare the Present Level page of the IEP before you meet with the IEP team if the student does qualify for the Resource Program.

Chapter 4

CURRICULUM ADJUSTMENTS

Resources Specialist competencies covered in Chapter 4: The Resource
Specialist must demonstrate—
1. the knowledge and appropriate use of district reading, language
   arts, math and social studies curriculum;
2. the knowledge and appropriate use of district-adopted materials
   in critical contest areas;
3. the knowledge of techniques used to modify and adapt regular
   curriculum and materials to meet individual student needs;
4. the ability to coordinate regular class materials and/or activities
   with remediation needs;
5. the knowledge of and ability to analyze district assessment
   procedures.

Curriculum adjustment is a very challenging part of the Resource Specialist's role. While there are a few guidelines that have proven effective, there are no set rules as to how to go about adjusting curriculum. Curriculum is adjusted to meet individual needs. For every student in a Resource Specialist Program you may have a different method of adapting the curriculum. Curriculum adjustments must also fit within the basic framework of the regular classroom teacher who has the RSP student in question. The adjusted curriculum must complement the regular teacher's plan or the whole purpose of adjusting curriculum is defeated. Curriculum adjustment is an ongoing process; it does not cease once you have outlined the U.S. History book for your RSP student. Your method of adjusting the curriculum for a student changes as the student grows and as his basic skills improve. You may find that you begin the school year making many extreme changes for a particular student in each of his classes. The new semester may find that fewer adjustments are required. By the end of the year his reading level may have risen to a point where he can read the regular test provided by the regular classroom teacher and, therefore, may require only minimal adjustments the following year.

The Resource Specialist at the elementary level places the main emphasis on remediating each student's specific learning disability. The philosophy is that if a student can bring this disability to age level or grade level, then this block to his learning will no longer prevent the student from working at grade level in the academic areas. Also, the elementary level is really the only practical level to attempt remediation of specific learning disabilities. At the secondary level, classroom teachers provide all students with the texts they are required to use. These texts are usually written at a level that is beyond the reading level of the RSP student. Therefore, Resource Specialists at this level are concerned with adapting the material so the RSP student can function in the regular classroom and learn the same material contained in textbooks he may not be able to read. The Resource Specialist may want to find an alternative text that will provide the same content material at a reduced reading level. The latter part of this chapter will list specific methods of seeking alternatives to textbooks too difficult for RSP students to read, as well as alternatives to the regular classroom curriculum.

There is little time, if any, for the secondary Resource Specialist to devote to the student's specific disability. If a student has trouble sequencing details, for example, this would have to be dealt with through the regular curriculum. An exercise in sequencing details could accompany each history chapter read. This is where the creative ability of the Resource Specialist is put to the true test, combining remediation with content area material.

As for developmental reading, the regular elementary classroom teachers have at their disposal a wide range of reading books and they are thus able to provide the RSP student with a reading book at the student's level. The same is true for the areas of math and spelling. The regular classroom teachers have a wide range of materials at their disposal, so they are better able to individualize these content areas to the level of the RSP student. This is not true at the secondary level. There may be one text available for the U.S. History class and quite possibly that book is not written at a remedial reading level. Recently, publishers presented content area textbooks written at remedial reading levels. Thus, it is the elementary Resource Specialist more than the secondary Resource Specialist who is able to concentrate on developing skills that are lacking in the RSP student. Examples of these skills are auditory memory, visual memory, fine-motor coordination, visual perceptual skills, sequencing, picking out the main idea, and drawing conclusions.

There are times, however, when the elementary Resource Specialist uses alternatives. In the intermediate grades, for example, the regular classroom teachers are provided with texts dealing with science and social studies. These texts are usually written at a higher reading level than that of the RSP student. Alternatives must be found so that the student can function in the regular classroom. This is also good preparation for the intermediate student, who will soon be in junior high or high school and will be faced with similar situations.

Not all regular classroom teachers will be enthusiastic about the prospect of students working on different assignments or out of different books at the same time, within one class. Care must be taken when making these adjustments so that the teacher will not feel imposed upon. Work together to try to design alternative assignments that will not only prove beneficial for the student but also decrease the teacher's anxiety level. Try to make the teacher understand that an alternative assignment will be less frustrating for the student, and if the student is less frustrated, the teacher is also less likely to be frustrated with the student. It may be extremely difficult in the beginning, but the rewards in the long run will certainly be worthwhile.

Many regular classroom teachers today are looking at modifications in a wholistic manner. That is, they are not just modifying specific assignments for certain students, but they are modifying their entire approach including delivery of information to the class. This approach includes the following components:

1. MODIFY—student behavior and organization skills;
2. ADAPT—lesson delivery, lesson content, method of student output;
3. REDUCE—quantity, speed, accuracy of student output;
4. CHANGE—test construction, evaluation mode, and grading system.

Here are certain criteria to keep in mind when designing alternative assignments for a student or deciding upon which teacher's classroom to place him in:

1. The student's learning characteristics and educational needs should be compatible with the learning environment in the regular classroom.
2. The student's learning characteristics and educational needs should be compatible with the regular classroom teacher's ability and willingness to modify instructional curriculum.
3. Special Education services must be supportive of the regular

classroom teacher's instructional goals and willing to assist the teacher in attempts to modify curriculum.

The remainder of this chapter is devoted to specific alternatives for the various content areas. In making curriculum adjustments, it is wise to keep a few important rules in mind:

1. Remember to fit the adjustment within the basic framework of the regular classroom teachers' plan; it is their material you are dealing with.
2. Keep in mind the student's strengths; don't tape a lecture if he has auditory problems; provide a written outline if his visual modality is strongest.
3. Ask the regular teacher for assistance, suggestions, or ideas; try to find alternatives together so you may both share the responsibility for the student's education.
4. Inform the parents and the student of the adjustments made and the reasons for making the adjustments; include these always in the IEP you have written for the student.
5. Keep a positive attitude; do not think something will not work until you have tried it. A positive attitude will easily transfer to your students and your colleagues at school.

There are available to the Resource Specialist specific methods of remediation by renowned educators. These methods may be used to comply with the objectives set forth in the student's IEP. Table III lists some of the more commonly used strategies and their area of emphasis.

Table III

CLASSROOM ALTERNATIVES

Classroom Organization	Classroom Management	Presentation Methods	Testing Methods	Resources
large group instruction	lecture	verbal lecture	verbal	visual aids
small group instruction	films	group discussion	written	worksheets
individual instruction	group discussion	film, audiovisuals	tape-recorded response	textbook
peer tutoring	homework	written work-sheets	fill-in	audio side
independent learning centers	tests	group activities	short answer	teacher prepared materials
cooperative learning groups	special projects	tape recorders	true/false	
teacher directed self-directed	*Reinforcers*	question/answer	matching	
	social praise		recognition/recall	
	notes home			
	privileges			
	grades			
	tangible rewards			
	PAT - Preferred Activity Time			

Content Area	Remedial Technique/Alternative	Source for Further Information	Elem	JH	SH
Reading Low sight vocabulary	Label objects and pictures around the room		X		
	Teach Dolch Word List	Dolch Word List	X	X	X
	Kinesthetic method/finger spelling	Fernald	X	X	X
	Word games		X	X	
	Clozure exercises -- making two lists of words, the first list complete and the second leaving letters out, have student fill in missing letter		X		
	Direct student to the smaller words in words		X	X	X
	Divide words into syllables		X	X	X

	Practice looking for the likenesses and differences in words by writing the word on the board and framing the like/unlike parts
	    like unlike
	  cook look cake cat				

	Instruction in the changes in words when endings are added		X	X	
	Rhyme exercises		X		
	Practice in enunciation and pronunciation (hearing it enunciated and pronounced correctly then having the student repeat)		X		
	Daily practice with Grope and Group cards		X	X	
	Use of Flashmeter to increase word recognition speed		X		
	Direct student toward the differences in letters -- their shape		X		

Reading

Content Area	Remedial Technique/Alternative	Source for Further Information	Elem	JH	SH
Low sight vocabulary	Develop spatial discrimination and left to right sequencing		X		
	Use word games that teach word attack skills		X		
	Keep a dictionary of new words, emphasizing alphabetical order				
	Flash card exercises				
	Instruction in the sounds of				
	consonants				
	blends				
	vowels				
	Maintain a display of picture word charts that change as new words are introduced into the students' vocabulary				
Fluency	Phrase reading exercises				
	Oral reading exercises				
	Use of easy material				
	Practice period of silent reading before oral reading		X	X	X
	Use of a tape recorder. The student can hear his own voice. Practice being a radio announcer or sports broadcaster into the tape recorder		X	X	
	Use of reading pacer		X		
	Promote as much self-confidence as possible; praise even for slight progress		X	X	
	Instruction in reading by thought units		X		

Content Area	Remedial Technique/Alternative	Source for Further Information	Elem	JH	SH
Reading					
Fluency	Practice choral reading using popular nursery rhymes or words to songs		X		
	Use of easy reading material with marked phrases		X		
	Have student read into a tape recorder then listen to himself as he reads along in the book		X		
	Instruction in scanning for difficult or unfamiliar words		X	X	X
	Instruction in correct left-right eye movement		X		
	Use of controlled reader		X		
	Use of marker to underline passage being read		X	X	X
Comprehension	Use of games, exercises, or worksheets that match words and pictures		X	X	X
	Exercises in summarizing paragraphs, chapters, small passages		X	X	X
	Exercises in outlining		X	X	X
	Practice listing major events in a paragraph, chapter, or small passage		X	X	X
	Exercise in detecting the sequence of events in a paragraph, chapter, or small passage		X	X	X
	Instruction in how to use context clues		X	X	X
	Instruction in drawing conclusions and making inferences		X	X	X
	Exercises in following oral and written directions		X	X	X

Content Area	Remedial Technique/Alternative	Source for Further Information	Elem	JH	SH
Reading Comprehension	Have students write up directions for each other, how to build a model or make something; concentrate on key words		X	X	X
	Exercises in clozure; present student with written passage at his reading level and omit every tenth word; pupil fills in the blank word		X	X	X
	SQ3R method of reading and study -- Survey Question Read Review Read again		X	X	X
	Use of Barnell Loft Specific Skills Series		X	X	X
	After reading a story, review the events before having individual students sequence the events themselves. This will help understand the flow of the story		X	X	X
	Have students underline the events in the story or write 1, 2, 3, etc. next to each event		X	X	X
	Exercise to teach signal sequence words -- first, second, then, next, last, soon, finally, after, later, the next day, etc.		X	X	X
Math	Cut math page in half to reduce amount of problems in one sitting (also helps the student with a short attention span; after finishing half the page in 20 minutes, he must get up and hand it in and get another half of the page; the walk to the teacher's desk absorbs some of his extra energy and reduces needless getting up out of his seat)		X	X	X

Content Area	Remedial Technique/Alternative	Source for Further Information	Elem	JH	SH
Math	Write out instead of type problems on the ditto		X	X	X
	Divide the paper into sections so the student has definite room in which to work and can learn to organize his work		X	X	X
	Reduce the number of problems or questions on a page		X	X	X
General Modifications Suitable to all Areas	Reduce the number of questions or items on a page		X	X	X
	Use large print materials		X	X	X
	When making dittos, use a primary typewriter or neatly print in large letters		X	X	
	Whenever possible, use yes/no or multiple choice answers on tests rather than sentence completion or essay		X	X	X
	Extra questions on the same idea should be added to enable the student to better understand the idea		X	X	X
	Phrase questions clearly		X	X	X
	Avoid questions that ask... "All of the following are correct except..." Many students read all are and ignore the except (this also deals with two concepts, which is confusing)		X	X	X
	Keep questions and phrases as brief as possible		X	X	X
	Use an outline format whenever possible. This highlights key information and reinforces outlining skills, which are necessary for junior and senior high school		X	X	X

Content Area	Remedial Technique/Alternative	Source for Further Information	Elem	JH	SH
General Modifications	Tape the textbook, weekly spelling lists, or tests*		X	X	X
	Provide clear and complete directions for each assignment. These may be given orally as well as visually		X	X	X
	Incorporate key content area words into weekly spelling lists		X	X	X
	Provide for progress checks so students are able to monitor their progress		X	X	X

* In California state adopted textbooks have tapes available at a limited fee (fee for the tape or you may send in your own tape)

Chapter 5

SURVIVAL AND STUDY SKILL

Resource Specialist competencies covered in Chapter 5: The Resource Specialist must demonstrate the ability to—
1. use and teach techniques that better enable students to retain information;
2. use and teach techniques that better enable students to cope with the pressures of school and achieve a more positive academic experience;
3. incorporate appropriate motivational techniques.

Adequate survival and study skills are essential for a successful school experience. These skills are usually taught with the regular classroom curriculum, but there are several reasons why RSP students have not always developed good study skills. One of the main reasons is that these students have often been excluded from the regular classroom to work on remediation skills in the RSP room. Another reason is the RSP students may not have adequately learned the concepts as taught in the regular classroom. Finally, students often have learning problems with respect to study skills such as organization, retention, sequencing and location. Therefore, it is imperative that these survival and study skills be taught in the RSP room and reinforced in the regular classroom.

There seems to be some overlap of necessary skills for students at the elementary, junior high and senior high school levels. Therefore, to avoid confusion, this chapter will discuss the specific survival and study skill areas and how these skills can be developed at the elementary, junior high and senior high school levels. The skill areas to be discussed are the following:

1. time management,
2. organization skills,
3. manipulative skills,
4. social skills,

5. fact-finding skills, and
6. test-taking skills.

TIME MANAGEMENT

At the elementary level not much homework is assigned to the students. Generally, what *is* assigned can be completed within twenty to thirty minutes. However, this is an excellent opportunity for the Resource Specialist to work with parents and regular classroom teachers to help the student develop good work habits. For instance, in the primary grades where very little, if any, homework is assigned, the regular class teacher and the Resource Specialist can develop support exercises for basic skills that the student can practice every day after school at a specific time.

At the junior and senior high levels it might be beneficial to have the student keep track of the amount of time needed to complete each assignment. This will reinforce the student's awareness of how to best manage time.

ORGANIZATIONAL SKILLS

This critical skill can set the pace for the student's entire future and is not just limited to the school setting. The key to becoming organized is to be structured yet flexible enough to handle change without falling apart. We have all seen the student who becomes anxious whenever his schedule is changed in any way. The student needs to be flexible enough to deal with these changes. Discussing the reason for and allowing the student to participate in the decision-making process leading to the change can help the student be more flexible. Another way to help the student is to teach basic organizational skills.

At the elementary level, the Resource Specialist can begin teaching organizational skills by having the student use a small flip-style pocket notebook to keep a daily record of homework assignments. In this way the student can check the notebook at the end of the day to see what books and materials are needed to finish the assignments at home. At home, after the student completes each assignment, he can mark out the entry in the notebook. If a student consistently fails to complete homework assignments, then a contract or reward system should be established. This can be phased out as the student begins to develop a feeling of reward by seeing his grades improve as a result of completing the assignments.

At the junior and senior high levels it is *essential* that the students have organizational skills. Now the student has to deal with five to six different teachers and classes. This entails adjusting to several different personalities, teaching styles, and a multitude of assignments.

Junior high students should be taught how to use a ring binder notebook with a section for each class, and how to keep a binder reminder or checksheet to record all homework assignments. The homework checksheet or binder reminder could easily be a carryover from the flip-style pocket notebook he learned to use at the elementary level.

Senior high students can further develop their organizational skills. They too should have a folder or notebook with sections for each class, and a special notebook checklist or form for recording the assignments given in class and their due dates. Take things a step further by giving the student a form to record the date, assignment, time spent on assignment and two checkoff columns: one labeled "completed" and the other labeled "need help." The RSP teacher should check these daily. Thus, the student can gain the satisfaction of keeping track of assignments, completing them, and being able to receive aid if confused rather than just giving up from frustration. The Resource Specialist also benefits from this record keeping by being able to better use the student's time in the Resource Specialist's classroom.

MANIPULATIVE SKILLS

Many students with learning problems also have fine motor difficulties. They need to acquire the ability to perform tasks that require them to use their hands to manipulate various objects.

For instance, at the elementary level it is imperative that the students be taught to handle scissors, pencils, and even to dress themselves in preparation for writing. When the student attends junior high school he may have to open a combination lock to keep books and materials in the assigned locker. There are companies that manufacture large, brightly colored plastic locks on which small children can practice. The older elementary student can practice on a real lock. Contact the local junior and senior high schools to see if the old locker doors beyond repair can be used by these elementary students for practice. If this skill has not been learned in the elementary grades, it will be necessary for the junior high Resources Specialist to teach this skill.

SOCIAL SKILLS

In order for a student to have a positive school experience, he must develop appropriate social skills. By social skills we mean learning the rules and regulations of the school and the classroom, society in general, as well as positive peer interaction. Students also need to be taught the consequences if rules and regulations are broken.

Usually the regular classroom teacher maintains a discipline program of some form. On occasion a teacher may fail to follow through with the consequences and the student may develop poor self-discipline. If this is the case for a student in RSP, then it is of vital importance that the Resource Specialist provide a discipline program or, possibly, that the Resource Specialist effect a classroom change to place the student in a more structured environment.

Upon entering junior high school the student learns very quickly that this school setting is definitely not like elementary school. All of a sudden there seems to be more people, more homework, more rules and more expectations. The student must know the school and the individual classroom rules. The consequences for noncompliance to these rules must also be made known and learned by the student. Knowing the reasons for rules and consequences for noncompliance encourages the student to behave in a positive manner, thus achieving a more positive school experience.

By the time the student reaches the senior high level, he should possess adequate social skills. If this is not the case, then the Resource Specialist can help the student to develop these skills. The restrictions and demands are much stronger at this level, and the student could easily become a school dropout if he has not learned to survive in the school setting by developing these skills.

FACT-FINDING SKILLS

This area is comprised of three components—survey skills, note-taking skills, and location skills. These three components are generally introduced at the elementary level, but their main importance becomes relevant at the junior and senior high levels.

Survey Skills —If the student is to experience any success, he must learn how to study and know exactly what to study. A common problem among students with learning problems is the difficulty in picking out important facts and details. The student should be able to pick out the main ideas and important events of a selection by skimming over the title of the selection and the key words within the selection. At the junior and senior high levels, little thought is given to assigning a student forty to fifty pages of reading a night from a combination of all his classes. This would be an extremely difficult task for the RSP student. As a Resource Specialist it is your job to help the student develop strategies to get through the material.

The SQ3R method is one of the most popular methods used to help students deal with material written at a slightly difficult reading level.

1. Survey—a rapid review of the introduction, summary, titles of each section, first sentence in each paragraph, and any visual aids provided;
2. Question—each section, turning the title into a question. For example, a section entitled "Causes of the Civil War" could be turned around to this question— "What were the causes of the Civil War?"
3. Read—reading each section in search of answers to the questions formulated in the above step;
4. Recite—answers to the questions should be written or recited in the student's own words;
5. Review—a written or oral statement of all that has been learned from the reading.

The student should then be able to outline the material read in brief outline form. This should have been taught at the elementary level, but often it is necessary to review or reteach this skill at the junior and senior high levels.

Note-Taking Skills —At the secondary level, most of the information given in class changes from reading (visual format) to lecture (auditory format). This change makes it very important for the student to develop listening and note-taking skills. Most students in the RSP program are at a disadvantage in this situation. Not only do they have difficulty with written expression, but many of these students may also have some level of auditory deficit. Sometimes an agreement can be worked out with the regular classroom teacher in which the student is allowed to use a tape recorder. Or, the teacher may allow the student to take notes from his own lecture notes or outline. Also, a "non-reading" student may pair up with a "note-taking" student and copy the notes from the "note-taking" student. However, if this is not possible, then the student will have to do his best taking his own notes. The student must be able to pick out the main ideas, decide what is relevant and what is not relevant. Who? What? When? Where? How? and Why? are important questions students should be able to answer when taking notes. Here are some suggestions to help teach or reinforce these note-taking skills:

1. Have the student bring in newspaper articles in which the specific questions, Who, What, When, Where, Why and How, have been answered and circle the sentences that answer these questions.

2. After class discussions, always have the student write down the main idea and key points discussed by the group.

3. Tape several classroom lectures and have the student practice taking notes from the recorded lesson.

4. Have your aide attend the regular class with the student and take notes from the instructor's lecture. Afterwards, the student and aide can compare notes to see if the student recorded the important information.

5. When answering questions at the end of chapters, teach students to identify questions as *RIGHT THERE;* meaning the answer is *right there* in the text in a few words, stated as the question is. For example:

QUESTION: What were the causes of . . .
RIGHT THERE ANSWER: The causes of . . . were . . .
LOOK FOR IT; meaning they may need to search the text for the answer and it may not be stated all in one sentence. For example:
QUESTION: What were the causes of . . .
LOOK FOR IT ANSWER: Many factors contributed to . . . One such factor was . . . Another factor was . . .
THINK ABOUT IT: Means the student needs to read the text and come to some conclusions about what was read or form some opinion from the information given.

Location Skills — The student needs to be taught textbook and reference material locational skills. The student also needs to know how to use the dictionary, encyclopedia, index, appendix and glossary of a book. These skills will be invaluable when reports and term papers are required at the secondary level.

TEST–TAKING SKILLS

This is an area that is not usually taught in the regular school curriculum, yet it does require a skill that can be taught to the RSP student to enhance performance on tests. Here are some suggestions to help the student have greater success when taking any kind of test:

1. Encourage students to ask the instructor what kind of test will be given (true/false, multiple choice, short answer, essay) and what will be emphasized on the test (notes, text, handouts, films); there is no need to use valuable study time on material that is not going to be on the test.

2. Help students establish regular study times to prevent cramming the night before the test.

3. Be sure the student can read and understand test terminology, e.g., define, clarify, compare, contrast, describe, compute, etc.

4. Encourage students to study prior tests to learn the types of questions asked.

5. Give the student mock tests to help him to follow the directions.

6. Resource Specialist should address the student's mental attitude before taking tests. Many times a student convinces himself that he will do poorly (self-fulfilling prophecy).

Many teachers encourage students to use a SCORER method. Each letter in the word stands for an important role in test taking.

S —Schedule your time! It is important to answer the easy questions first. Mark the unanswered questions and then it takes very little time to locate them when going back to answer these harder questions.

C —Clue words. The word *rarely* usually indicates an incorrect answer, whereas the words *usually* and *sometimes* frequently indicate correct answers. Other clue words are *all, same, never.*

O —Omit the difficult questions. If the question is one you do not know, do not waste time trying to figure out a way to answer it. Skip the question, and if you have any time left after answering all the other questions, then return to it and attempt to write an answer.

R — Read carefully, especially the directions, to avoid careless mistakes.

E —Estimate the answer. If a test is devised such that a student is not penalized for guessing at questions he is not sure of, then the student should try to estimate which answer is the most likely to be correct.

R — Review the answers. Always review the answers, but do not be in a hurry to change them because the first choice has the greater likelihood of being the correct answer.

Taking essay tests requires the student to have a broad understanding of the subject matter. The RSP student needs to use organizational skills carefully in order to answer essay questions, for the most important component in completing an essay test is careful planning. The student needs to plan (outline) what needs to be written so as to answer the question sufficiently. One suggestion is to use the majority of the allotted time planning the answer. For example, if thirty minutes are given to answer the question, then some time should be spent on planning as well as on the actual writing. This would help the student organize his thoughts and still adequately answer the question. It might also be helpful for the student to write down all that can be remembered from studying so that the student does not "blank out" when answering the question.

There are other options the Resource Specialist can take. One alternative would be to check with the regular classroom teacher to see if the student could be allowed to answer the question in outline form, or perhaps the teacher might consent to an oral examination. Another option would be for the Resource Specialist to give the test in the RSP classroom or have the student at least finish the exam in the RSP classroom if the time provided in the regular classroom is not sufficient.

Teaching survival skills is just as important to student success as learning to read, write, and do math.

Chapter 6

DISCIPLINE

Resource Specialist competencies covered in Chapter 6: The Resource
Specialist must demonstrate the ability to—
1. establish rules for providing a positive learning environment,
   logical consequences for infractions of these rules, and provide
   reward/reinforcement for appropriate behaviors;
2. use the school's discipline policies and enlist parental support for
   developing appropriate behaviors;
3. select the target behavior for modification, develop methods to
   reinforce desired behavior, and provide rewards for appropriate
   behaviors;
4. use the administration, staff, parents, and peers in a behavior
   management program.

Discipline is a vital part of any school program. For any learning to
occur, teachers must have a certain amount of control in their
classroom, whether this is informal or formal in nature. The Resource
Specialist must not only have strong classroom control but must also be
knowledgeable of various discipline techniques to suit the needs of
individual students who may need more direct intervention. The discipline policy of the Resource Specialist Program should correlate closely
with that of the regular classroom teachers for two reasons: (1) so that
there will be an easier transition in mainstreaming students, and (2) so
that consistency is maintained for the already mainstreamed students
between the Resource Specialist Program and the regular teacher's
program. When it is evident that a student is in need of an individualized discipline program because he cannot survive under the regular
discipline program, then the regular classroom teacher should be brought
in on the planning. The behavior should then be worked on where the
student is spending most of his time, which is usually the regular
classroom, unless the behavior is exhibited only in the Resource Specialist's
room.

The regular teacher must handle many behavior problem students in the classroom, some of whom might be RSP students or candidates. The Resource Specialist often will be asked to observe a student as a possible referral or just to assist the teacher with a student who is a disruptive influence in the classroom. The following are points to remember and questions to answer when observing a student's behavior in the classroom:

1. Don't be obtrusive. Come into the classroom after the bell has rung and sit in the back of the room. Make a note as to where the child is seated in the classroom. Often a change in seating arrangement can work wonders.

2. Before observing the student, be sure to have background information such as the student's history of significant behavior problems, possible difficulties at home, peer relationships, or the demands of the classroom.

3. Have the teacher document the behavior precisely. The teacher should cite the specific behaviors that the student is exhibiting that are not appropriate for the classroom. The teacher should ask herself whether this is a teacher problem or a student problem.

4. What is the general classroom environment like: Is the classroom organized? Are the desks crammed together, or do the students have ample work space? Are the students given structure, or are they encouraged to be self-directed? Does the teacher use various teaching methods, or does she only use one style when another might be more beneficial to the student in question?

5. How does the teacher interact with the student? Is the teacher comfortable when working with the students? Do the students have an accepting attitude towards the teacher, the curriculum, and the other students in the class?

6. What are the rules for classroom behavior? Are they specified? Do the students understand the rules and the consequences? Are the rules realistic? Can the teacher be flexible or does she demand total compliance with no exceptions?

7. What has the teacher already tried in order to modify inappropriate behavior? Specifically, what ideas did not work and why?

8. How does the student relate to his peers? Does he appear to be liked or disliked by the majority? Does he associate with other students that are consistently in trouble? Does he use his behavior to seek acceptance from his peers?

9. Observations should take place during direct instruction. Does the

student understand what the teacher is saying? Note the behavior that is exhibited during direct instruction.

10. How does the student use independent work time? The student may not have the self-control to work independently without some guidance. Are the assignments of an unreasonable length?

11. By observation and conversation with the teacher, find out what the student likes to do in the classroom or at school. This should be included in recommendations made to the teacher or in an IEP meeting.

12. Sometimes the suggestions made to the regular classroom teacher and the approaches used in the Resource Specialist's room have proven ineffective. At this time, it may be helpful to bring in the school psychologist as another resource. The student may be having psychological problems that one is not aware of or able to assess at this time. Although you have expertise in many areas, it is important to use the auxiliary personnel, for they have expertise in different areas and often suggest fresh approaches.

After answering these questions, a great deal of information has been gathered about the variables that are affecting the student's behavior. If this was an informal consultation and it is felt that learning deficits may be present, then a recommendation might be made to assess the student for the Resource Specialist's Program. If it is felt, however, that the inappropriate behavior is not due to or causing a learning disability and academic difficulty, then the Resource Specialist might give the teacher some suggestions for remediation of the problem. It is important to remember that the Resource Specialist is a consultant, and the problem-solving phase should be conducted as a joint effort between the Resource Specialist and the regular classroom teacher.

There are many discipline programs that can be used in the classroom. The first step in developing a discipline program for the classroom is to decide on rules. A good way to do this is by listing behaviors that can and cannot be tolerated. The rules will develop naturally from the behavior that cannot be tolerated. Think about what is needed in terms of student behavior in order to do your job—teach. It's a good idea to make these few in number. Try to keep it down to no more than five, otherwise all the time is spent "policing" and minimal time is spent instructing.

After developing the classroom rules, the next step is to examine the logical consequences that result from breaking the rules. These consequences usually range from warnings to withholding privileges, from parent contacts to administrative discipline policies. Each teacher should pick consequences that she can and will enforce. Posting the rules and consequences in the classroom prevents misunderstandings from occurring. Another suggestion is to have the student and the parents sign a contract that states the rules and consequences. Always include the parents in individual discipline programs so that both the home and the school are striving for the same goal. The more support one has from home, the better the program will work.

The final step involved in developing a discipline program is to decide on the rewards or reinforcers for appropriate behaviors. These can range from concrete, tangible rewards such as stars, points, special privileges, free time, and food to social rewards such as praise, notes, smiles, improved grades, and success in the classroom. There is no one specific reward or reinforcer that works every time or even the majority of the time. In fact, the best results are obtained if the student helps decide on the reward or reinforcer for incentive. This is especially true at the secondary level.

It is imperative that each teacher research the discipline program the school uses. If there is no schoolwide plan, the teacher needs to develop her own program, but it is wise to clear the program with the site administrator before implementation.

It is also very important to inform the student's parents of the discipline program either by personal contact (conferences, phone call) or by written contact (note, contract). Doing this can prevent misunderstandings in the future and often results in enlisting the parents' support if contacts are necessary to maintain the norm in the classroom. Of course, any time a parent contact takes place, it should be documented.

Occasionally, a student has one or more behaviors that do not meet expectations of the teacher. In the event that this occurs, the discipline program usually is not sufficient to deal with the inappropriate behavior, and a behavior management contract needs to be developed.

The initial step in developing a behavior management contract is to decide on *one* target behavior to modify. Often there is more than one behavior needing change, so try to pick the one that is most inappropriate or annoying. Remember, this should be a behavior that affects the learning environment and not something that is just personally irritating. It is also important to remember to work only on one behavior at a time. To do more may cause confusion and conflict. Much concentrated effort on the part of the student and teacher is needed to effect a change in behavior, so do not thwart the efforts by trying to change too many behaviors at one time.

After deciding on the target behavior, the next step is to develop the method for reinforcing appropriate behaviors. Once again, involving the student in this process results in greater success. Informing the student of the problem behavior, why it is a problem, and asking the student for help in changing the behavior builds a foundation for trust between the student and teacher, positively increases a student's self-concept when he knows he can have control over the behavior, and, since the student is taking responsibility for his own actions, develops maturity.

The final step is for the student and the teacher to agree on the reward for achieving appropriate behavior. This should be something meaningful to the student, something that is of *value* to the student, not something that the teacher thinks would be a nice reward. If it does not hold significance for the student, then success is improbable and frustration results for both the teacher and the student.

Whenever a behavior management contract is initiated, it is imperative that the site administrator and the student's parents be informed of the complete program. If there is any disagreement about the program, the time to straighten it out is before, not after, implementation. This eliminates misunderstandings and promotes strong support. It is also a good idea to inform any other teachers who deal with the student of the developed contract. This way they can support and follow through to further reinforce the desired behavior change.

The most important aspect of both the discipline contract and the behavior management program is *consistency*. If the teacher is consistent with the developed program, the students quickly learn their limits, learn that the teacher treats everyone fairly, and a harmonious learning environment is quickly established. If a teacher is not consistent, the usual result is constant debating about the teacher's actions. The teacher is then drawn into defending herself. This could have easily been avoided if the teacher were just consistent in following the established program.

Of course, there is always one student who is the exception to the rule. When a teacher is confronted with a situation in which the established program does not apply, then the situation should be handled as fairly and diplomatically as possible.

The following are brief summaries of several specific discipline and behavior management programs.

ASSERTIVE DISCIPLINE

Assertive Discipline is based upon the reality of potential positive influence that teachers can have on the behavior of their students. Through Assertive Discipline teachers can learn to "take charge" of their classroom in a firm, yet positive manner. This approach does not advocate teachers storming into the classroom and "throttling" any student who opens his mouth. What it does advocate is that teachers need to set firm, consistent limits while remaining cognizant of the student's need for warmth and positive support. The main steps involved in this program are to establish classroom rules, continually provide positive feedback for appropriate behaviors, and, most of all, *be consistent.*

REALITY TRAINING

This approach calls for the student to make realistic decisions when confronted with a problem. The assumptions that form the rationale for Reality Therapy are as follows: Each person is responsible for his own behavior. The terms "mentally ill" and "incapable" are avoided because they have a tendency to excuse behavior. The individual's personal history relating to his problem is of no interest. The present and future are all that matter in dealing with behavior. Behaviors are not excused based on unconscious motivation. Emphasis is given to the morality of behavior. There are no transference figures. Teachers relate to the student with a problem as themselves. Socially accepted ways are taught to students so as to fulfill their needs.

Reality Therapy requires special training. This training can be obtained by attending one of the workshops held frequently around the country. This is not usually done in elementary or intermediate grades.

LIFE SPACE INTERVIEWS

This program was designed for professionals to use with individuals in crises situations. The program employs an interview technique. The teacher conducts and directs the interview, listens carefully to the student's responses, and helps the student make a decision as to how the crisis should be handled. When a crisis arises the teacher follows the following Life Space Interview steps. Each student involved in the crisis relates his own impression of what has happened. The teacher listens and makes sure each student has the chance to describe the situation without interruption. Students are then questioned by the teacher to determine the actual cause of the disturbance. After the students finish describing their perception of the problem, the teacher will help determine the accuracy of their perception. The student must then suggest ways to resolve the situation. If a solution is agreed upon by all persons involved, the Life Space Interview stops. If there is no agreeable solution, the teacher takes a more active role. The realities of the situation are defined, and the consequences of the behavior are spelled out. The teacher then begins to make suggestions on ways to solve this problem. The last step in this process is the development of a plan that may be used if the problem should arise again. The students should play a major role in deciding on this contingency plan.

The approach is much like Reality Therapy in that the student makes realistic decisions when confronted with a problem. This program's strongest point is that it provides specific guidelines for handling any crisis that might arise in the classroom.

ROLE PLAYING OR SOCIODRAMA

This technique encourages students to play certain roles in acting out problems in a problem situation as they perceive it. This can be followed up with a discussion when a group of students are involved to help clarify certain aspects of roles that were played. This program may be especially useful in helping the mainstreamed student handle peer relationships in the regular classroom.

VALUES CLARIFICATION

This program is a commonly used approach designed to help students build their own value system. Students actively learn about their own feelings and behaviors when considering their belief systems. The teacher gives the student the opportunity to make choices and encourages the student to evaluate the consequences of the choices. This approach also helps to build a student's self-confidence.

SKILL STREAMING

This is an approach to behavior management that looks at appropriate behavior as an entity that can be taught to students who do not appear to demonstrate appropriate behavior. The foundation of a skill-building approach is based on communication and modeling of expected and appropriate behavior along with consequences and accountability.

This is a very brief outline of some of the more commonly used behavior management systems. Each teacher will need to decide which will fit into her classroom plan. One system may be used exclusively, or parts of several may be incorporated into one plan. This will depend upon the personality of the teacher as well as her students and may vary from time to time. A behavior management plan of some form should be developed to insure an optimum and positive learning environment for the class.

BIBLIOGRAPHY

1. Canter, L. and Canter, M.: *Assertive Discipline.* Los Angeles, Canter & Associates, 1976.
2. Glasser, W.: *Reality Therapy: A New Approach to Psychiatry.* New York: Harper and Row, 1965.
3. Hammill, D. and Bartel, N.: *Teaching Children with Learning and Behavior Problems.* Boston, Allyn and Bacon, 1978.
4. Kohfildt, J.: *Contracts.* New York, Innovative Educational Support Systems, 1964.
5. Norris, R.J.: *Behavior Modification with Children.* Cambridge, Massachusetts, Winthrop Pub., Inc., 1976.
6. Raths, L., Harmin, M., and Simon, S.: *Values and Teaching.* Columbus, Ohio, Merrill, 1968.
7. Rauch, S.: *Handbook for the Volunteer Tutor.* Newark, Delaware, International Reading Association, 1969.
8. Redl, F.: The Concept of Life Space Interviewing.
9. Long, N., Mores, W., and Newman, R.: *Conflict in the Classroom.* Belmont, California, Wadsworth, 1971.
10. Shaftel, F.R. and Shafter, G.: *Role-Playing for Social Values: Decision Making in Social Studies.* Englewood Cliffs, New Jersey, Prentice-Hall, 1967.
11. Simon, S.B., Howe, L.W., and Kirchenbaum, H.: *Values Clarification.* New York, Hart, 1972.
12. Wiederhold, L.J., Hammill, D.D., and Brown, V.: *The Resource Teacher: A Guide to Effective Practices.* Boston, Allyn and Bacon, 1978.

Chapter 7

TIME MANAGEMENT

Resource Specialist competencies covered in Chapter 7: The Resource Specialist must demonstrate the ability to—
1. schedule her time to effectively perform all required duties;
2. schedule students needing daily RSP services and those needing intermittent instructional service;
3. organize instructional materials in the RSP room for easy access by aides, regular classroom teachers and students;
4. schedule testing time;
5. schedule conference and consultation time.

The successful operation of any classroom requires careful planning and organization on the part of the teacher. This is especially true for the Resource Specialist.

Previous chapters have discussed the importance of accurate record keeping and consistent communication. Time management is an equally important skill that must be developed to maintain a successful Resource Specialist Program.

The Resource Specialist must carefully plan time to include these three duties:

1. the scheduling of students on a daily or as-needed basis for direct instructional service by the Resource Specialist;
2. the scheduling of assessment of students referred to the Resource Specialist as well as annual assessment of identified students in the program;
3. the scheduling of consultation and planning time.

CLASS SCHEDULING

Scheduling students in the RSP program can be a very challenging experience. There are several approaches to scheduling, and the Resource Specialist will probably use more than one in her planning. No matter which scheduling method is used, scheduling must reflect the needs of the students as much as possible. There are of course times when it will be impossible to do this. There will always be the student who should be in RSP third period so that he can be in a group of seventh graders all at his ability level, but that is the only time he can get into World History with a teacher using the lower reading level history book.

The grouping of students according to their ability is probably the most desirable method of scheduling, although it is not often possible. By scheduling students according to their ability, the Resource Specialist can spend more time working with the students' deficiencies. Students can get more attention when in a class with other students having the same needs.

At the elementary level, the readiness and basic skills can be taught while strengthening the deficiencies. At the secondary level there seems to be little time, if any at all, for reinforcement of deficit areas. However, skill grouping allows time for this while concentrating on the content areas. If there are a number of ninth graders reading at a fourth to fifth grade level who could be scheduled into RSP at the same time, they could strengthen their reading while learning history. The Resource Specialist may first need to substitute the regular textbook with one (on the same subject matter) written at a lower reading level. The reading of the text could be done as a group or by listening to a taped version of the text, followed by a discussion. If there are questions to be answered following each chapter, they could be designed to strengthen weak areas such as vocabulary, sequencing events, getting the main idea and drawing conclusions. Many publishers have used this format in textbooks that have been designed for Special Education or students with lower reading levels. The Resource Specialist would want to coordinate the lessons with those lessons planned by the regular classroom teacher.

Skill grouping may present a problem for the student who has difficulty accepting his learning problem. You would not want to place such a sixth grader with fourth graders even though his reading level may be comparable to their third grade reading ability. The embarrassment felt by the student may only hinder any academic remediation that could possibly take place.

Students can also be scheduled into RSP as little as one period per week. Students may only need RSP assistance when taking a test. Some students may need to see the Resource Specialist for supplemental or support exercises for concepts taught in the regular classroom. Some schools have a daily silent reading period. During this time, RSP students may come to the Resource Specialist for extra support.

When scheduling students on an as-needed basis such as this, it is wise to include the regular classroom teacher in your plans. Each teacher feels that her class is important, and she does not want students to miss anything she has to offer. The best way to gain that teacher's support is to explain that you are trying to assist her with these students. Plan a time together when you can see the student to give extra help and listen to any suggestions the teacher may offer.

Math Teacher:	Michael is so lost in math. He just cannot keep up, and I cannot hold up the whole class just because of him.
Resource Specialist:	Do you think he could keep up if he had another hour or so of help each week?
Math Teacher	I think so. Once he catches on he seems to do fine. It just takes so much extra explanation for him to catch on, and I cannot afford the time.
Resource Specialist	How much time in class is given to group instruction?
Math Teacher	About fifteen or twenty minutes, and then the students work on their own. What they do not complete in class they finish for homework. I usually give two or three pages a day, and most students finish two in class and have one for homework. Mike can only get about three pages done all week!
Resource Specialist	How about sending Michael to me after you give the instruction? While the rest of the class is working silently I can give him extra explanation before he begins his worksheets. He will not be embarrassed to ask questions because his classmates, who all seem to understand, will not be around to hear.
Math Teacher	That way we will know for sure that he understands the assignment, but he is still so slow.
Resource Specialist	Yes, he is slow. Now, do we want him to complete three pages of math each day or learn how to add fractions?
Math Teacher	Add fractions, of course! Isn't it unfair though to

	the other students who have to do three pages daily?
Resource Specialist	Is it fair to Michael to spend three hours daily doing what most students can do in an hour?
Math Teacher	I see! Let's give him one page and see how he does. If his speed picks up we can always add a page.
Resource Specialist	Congratulations! You have just individualized your math class. Without the pressure of getting through three agonizing pages of math each night, Michael may be able to concentrate more on the one page and be more successful.

This dialogue has actually made two points. First, it illustrates how this staggered or as-needed scheduling can be accomplished. It also is a good example of how curriculum adjustments can be made.

The math teacher in this dialogue is one you will want to do business with again. You will definitely want your students in his class. Do not forget to let your principal know how cooperative that teacher has been.

Probably the most common way to schedule students into RSP is one of the least favorable ways. This is the RSP room that contains several students of different grade levels all working on different assignments at one time! The Resource Specialist needs roller skates. It is not at all uncommon in an elementary room such as this to find more than one reading group going on all at once. Similarly, in a secondary RSP room, you may find groups of students working on two or more different history lessons, several math assignments, and various shop, science, and homemaking activities, all going on at the same time. And everyone needs help! To add to this, students continually drop in to take tests or ask questions. This is when your aide will be a great asset. It is hoped that your aide will be able to give tests or work with small groups of students. Even student aides can be used to tutor on a one-to-one basis.

Any or all of these methods may be used when scheduling RSP students. These methods can be combined or modified to best suit the needs of the students, regular classroom teachers and Resource Specialist.

SCHEDULING TESTING TIME

In addition to scheduling students, the Resource Specialist must set aside enough time to allow for adequate assessment of referred students.

Since there are a limited amount of school days from the date parent permission is received, it is wise to begin the testing as soon as possible. Testing time must coordinate with the student's schedule as well as the Resource Specialist's. When scheduling testing time there are a few points to consider.

1. Mondays or the first day back from vacation are not usually optimum times to test.
2. Friday will find both student and examiner tired from the week's work and will therefore probably not be an optimum testing day.
3. The last period of the day is a very poor time to test.
4. The period following PE may find the student too "wound up" for testing. However, the period preceding PE may be a good time to test, as the student can unwind after the test during PE.
5. The first period of the day may not find some students alert enough for testing, while for others this may be the best time.
6. It is not recommended to test a student when you have other students in the room.

Students in RSP must also be re-evaluated each year. Some districts evaluate all students each spring. Other districts re-evaluate students on their birthdays, while others re-evaluate on the student's entry date into RSP. There are advantages and disadvantages for each method. Each Resource Specialist must follow the guidelines established by the district and fit this into the total planning calendar.

YEARLY PLANNING CALENDAR

In the Fall. When scheduling students to come to the RSP room, at the elementary level, it is a good idea to coordinate the time for students that are shared with the Speech and Language Pathologist.

Also, it is a good idea to check with the regular classroom teachers to see if there is a block of time that would be more convenient for the student to come to RSP. Ideally, it is best to see students for reading during their reading period and math during their math time, but this is not always possible.

The groups of students should ideally number no more than eight at a time. Depending on the classroom size or the abilities of your aide(s), you might want to keep groups as low as possible. It is also helpful to group students by ability levels and disability area to facilitate your daily schedule and planning. Again, this is not always possible.

It is required by law to provide the regular classroom teacher with a copy of the student's IEP (-ref.-AB 3043, Chapter 1373). Thus, it is a good idea to explain the IEP and what the components mean. Also, it is helpful to review the IEP with the regular classroom teacher, to coordinate efforts, and to provide knowledge of what to expect from your instruction. Often the regular classroom teacher will ask the RSP teacher to reinforce a specific skill that the student is learning in the regular classroom. This can be addressed in the IEP.

In the Spring. Some districts allow the RSP teacher to take one to two weeks for year-end evaluations, but generally the school districts require the RSP teacher to conduct annual reviews consistent with the IEP date. Evaluations need to be conducted during the hours scheduled for assessment, conferences, planning, paperwork, etc.

At the elementary level, it is a good idea to write a brief history of the students that are moving on to the secondary level so as to share what has been successful with the student as far as motivation, behavior, etc. It is needless to let all the hard work be thrown out when the following teacher can get the student off to a good start with the information from the elementary input.

Throughout the Year. There are several tasks that need to be handled all year long including writing and updating IEPs, child study meetings, annual reviews, three-year reviews, and scheduling conferences and parent group meetings.

When reviewing the IEPs during the annual review, the Resource Specialist might decide that a student is ready for dismissal from the program. If this is the case, then the Resource Specialist needs to be able to show documentation that the student no longer requires the services of the program and have a plan for re-entry into the mainstream.

Also, teachers, parents, principals, etc., are continuously referring students for possible placement in RSP. Thus, the Resource Specialist is responsible for assessing these students to see whether or not they qualify for RSP. If they qualify, the Resource Specialist needs to take the necessary steps to enroll the student into the program.

Often the Resource Specialist will be called upon to conduct in-service training for teachers and/or parents. Informally, they may consult with regular classroom teachers to help them modify their own instructional techniques or lesson plans. The implementation of Section 504 (Rehabilitation Act) may involve the Resource Specialist in assisting with the development of Accommodation Plans for individual students who may or may not also qualify for Special Education services.

Careful planning is a vital aspect of the Resource Specialist Program. A person who is not very organized personally may encounter difficulty carrying out the responsibilities of the Resource Specialist if the job is not approached in an organized and thoughtful manner. Teacher preparation institutions and many districts offer courses in this type of organizational preparation. It will be difficult enough to teach the RSP students to be organized and careful planners. If we ourselves are not organized, it may be impossible to teach this skill to our students.

Chapter 8

COPING WITH PRESSURE

Resource Specialist competencies covered in Chapter 8: The Resource
Specialist must demonstrate the ability to—
1. identify aspects of the program that can create stress;
2. recognize symptoms associated with stress and burnout;
3. identify stress breakers.

Working in a situation as complex as a Resource Specialist Program
can be extremely demanding and may bring with it many pressures.
If these pressures are not dealt with properly, burnout may occur. Burnout is the physical and/or emotional exhaustion that can result from a
demanding position. Burnout is actually stress that has gotten out of
control.

This chapter will identify some of the causes of stress for the RSP
teacher. It will then determine different ways to prevent stress from
happening. Finally, suggestions will be offered for eliminating these
symptoms should they already be present.

The following is a list of some of the more common causes of stress for
the RSP teacher.

1. lack of administrative support/cooperation,
2. lack of parent support/cooperation,
3. lack of student effort/cooperation,
4. demands to be flexible,
5. demands from the staff,
6. dealing with severe behavior problems,
7. dealing with academic/learning problems,
8. dealing with students' physical problems,
9. dealing with students' emotional problems,
10. dealing with frustrated, angry, or upset parents,
11. pressure created because the staff regards the RSP position as an
    easy one with only a dozen or so students to deal with at one time,
12. the tremendous amount of paperwork,

63

13. continual changes in the program brought about by continual changes in legislation,
14. teaching several subjects at once,
15. having to be in more than one place at once,
16. numerous parent/staff conferences,
17. a feeling that you have to solve all the students' problems,
18. risk of budget cuts and layoffs.

BURNOUT INDICATORS

Burnout does not happen overnight or even over the weekend. It may seem as though it hits overnight but is actually accompanied by certain symptoms lasting an indefinite period of time. Burnout symptoms may be categorized as physical, behavioral or emotional.

Physical Symptoms

The physical symptoms are probably the most obvious. They may manifest themselves as:
1. gastrointestinal problems
2. body aches, primarily head, neck and back
3. inability to fall asleep at night and stay asleep
4. increased need for sleep
5. increase in the amount of colds, sore throat symptoms or other physical ailments

The physical symptoms are the most obvious, and the sufferer rarely views them as indicators of stress. The symptoms are treated as merely that, and the cause of them goes undetermined. The symptoms may disappear for awhile but will probably recur at a later date. If the stress creating these symptoms is extreme, the symptoms may persist and arouse the need to seek the help of a physician. But again, a doctor may treat the symptom and let the actual cause go untreated.

Mr. H., the RSP teacher at the high school, found himself listening to all the teachers complain about the inappropriate behavior of one of the RSP students. This became a daily habit. After promising the teachers at each one of these sessions that he would talk to the student, Mr. H. would quietly go back to his office and pop an antacid tablet into his mouth to try to calm his upset stomach. The student's behavior deteriorated along with Mr. H.'s stomach. At an in-service workshop on stress, Mr. H. came to realize that the problems he was having with this student were causing his stomach pains. The director of the in-service workshop helped Mr. H. devise a behavior modification plan that each teacher could easily use with the student in the classroom and report to Mr. H. each week instead of daily. The plan was implemented and was successful from the start. The student began to behave more appropriately, and to Mr. H.'s surprise, his stomach pains began to disappear.

A similar stressful situation could be causing another teacher to have trouble sleeping at night. Taking sleeping pills will only help you sleep, treat the symptom, and do nothing for the cause.

Ms. M. was a first year teacher as well as a new Resource Specialist. Her college courses did not prepare her for the multitude of daily tasks she was required to accomplish. Despite her detailed planning, she found herself lying awake at night going over in her mind what she would do the next day. She found her job even more difficult to perform after such a sleepless night. Burnout symptoms were beginning to occur before the first quarter was even over. Her principal, a very organized person, noticed her coming to school looking as if she had been up all night. The principal mentioned this to Ms. M. and was told about Ms. M.'s dilemma. The principal made a very helpful suggestion. Each night before bed make a list for the next day. Use two columns: "Things I Must Do" and "Things I Will Try To Do." List only the critical tasks in the "Must Do" column, and cross them out as each is accomplished. Leave the list next to the bed in case you do wake up in the middle of the night thinking about something you forgot to list. Write it down immediately so you can get back to sleep. Ms. M. tried this and felt relieved immediately. Her tasks did not seem quite so overwhelming now that she had learned to identify exactly what needed to get done each day. She also found that she was soon able to accomplish more of the tasks in the "Try To Do" column.

Behavioral Symptoms

Behavioral symptoms manifest themselves under the guises of alcohol, food, and drugs, and these may bring about changes in personality. A casual drink after work to unwind may quickly turn into a dangerous situation for the teacher under stress and on the verge of burnout. Drugs have also been used either to get the teacher going in the morning or as a relaxer in the evening. This is not only harmful to the body, but it does nothing to solve the teacher's actual problems. The same problems bothering Mr. H. and Ms. M. in the previous case studies may manifest themselves in other teachers in the form of drugs, food, or alcohol, and create changes in their personality. Similar action to that of Mr. H. and Ms. M. may be taken by the teacher indulging in food, alcohol or drugs. However, often excessive use of these occur before the teacher realizes that it has in itself become another problem. Now the teacher not only has a problem because of the stress created at school, but she has developed a dependency on drugs, alcohol, or food as well. In addition to offering workshops on stress management, many districts are beginning to realize the increase of substance abuse among their teachers and are establishing programs to assist teachers suffering from this. The teacher whose stress has brought her to this point is now in need of professional help and should seek it as soon as possible.

Emotional Symptoms

Depression, boredom, resentment, and frustration are all emotional symptoms of extreme stress or burnout. These can accompany the more obvious physical symptoms. The teacher who has become depressed about her school situation may easily become depressed about other aspects of life. Emotional symptoms affect every part of daily life and may therefore be much more difficult to bring under control.

It is necessary to recognize these symptoms as signs of something far more serious than a mere headache, a slight drinking problem or pre-menstrual depression. They are definite indicators of stress and if not dealt with can easily and quickly lead to serious physical and mental health problems. The longer the stressful situation goes untreated, the greater the toll your body pays and the harder it is to bring the problem under control.

STRESS BREAKERS

Once the source has been determined, it is necessary to look at all possible stress breakers. Stress breakers are activities that are meant to relax the mind and body, thus interrupting the stressful situation. This is not to say that everyone who participates in any of these activities will be immune to stress and burnout. There is no immunity for stress. Simply, these activities are meant to try to reduce the risk of stress and burnout. There are a multitude of stress breakers, and this is not meant to be a comprehensive list. Each teacher will have to select for herself which are likely to be pleasant and effective. The following is a suggested list of possible stress breakers.

athletic

tennis	volleyball	roller skating
softball	ice skating	handball
swimming	racquetball	jogging
bicycling	weight lifting	exercising
walking	dancing	jumping rope

creating

reading	painting	sewing
music	cooking	drawing
crocheting	needlepoint	knitting

miscellaneous

yoga	jacuzzi	massage
meditation	gardening	sauna
biofeedback	photography	collecting things

some other stress breakers

1. take a walk the same time each day,
2. cut down on caffeine intake,
3. take a class just for fun,
4. work out in a gym,
5. plan regular daily exercise,
6. set aside thirty minutes each day for yourself and tell everyone to stay away, this is your time,
7. put some energy into housework or chopping up a healthy green salad,
8. take a nap,
9. take a mental health day every now and then for yourself.

REMEMBER: the responsibility is yours and yours alone. No one else can do this for you, and you are of no help to others if you are burnt out and not happy with yourself.

Finding the time for these stress breakers presents a problem in itself. Everyone knows that RSP teachers have enough work to keep them busy for at least twenty-four hours a day. However, just as carefully as you plan your students' IEPs, you must take equal care and time to plan for yourself. It may require a whole day to sit down and design priorities in your life. Throw out those things in your life that are not needed at this time. Just as you throw out old clothes every few years, throw out unwanted aspects of your daily life. Make a chart, daily, weekly and monthly. Plan some time each day for yourself. Plan something for that time and follow through with it. These are some ideas you may want to incorporate into your planning.

1. Tell others about your plan so family and colleagues will not interfere (of course, you probably will not want to plan your personal quiet time at dinner time or other busy times; be reasonable in your planning).
2. Make daily lists of things that must get done; do not make your list too lengthy.
3. Check out the balance of your life and make alterations where necessary; set aside time for self, work, family, friends.
4. Assign priorities to your needs and wants.
5. Assign priorities to your activities.
6. Plan time for phone calls, trips to the market, minor emergencies.
7. Take vacations, mini or maxi.
8. Do something on the spur of the moment (remember when you used to be so spontaneous?).
9. Check the newspaper for entertainment ideas and cultural events.
10. Smell the air as you leave for work each day; look at the sky and feel the air.
11. Tell your students that you are undertaking this new plan and incorporate them into your schedule.
12. Evaluate your plan every now and then; add new activities and delete ones that are not so enjoyable.

The multitude of responsibilities demanded of the RSP teacher will continue to create stressful situations. As long as the RSP teacher is able to identify the causes of stress and incorporate stress breakers into daily life, effectiveness will be maintained on the job as well as in personal life.

GLOSSARY OF TERMS

Burnout: the physical and/or emotional exhaustion that can occur after a few years (or months in some cases) in a demanding professional or personal role; also, stress that has gotten out of control.

Caregiver: one who consistently gives help or assistance to others.

Distress: physical and/or emotional strain.

Energy Booster: a person or situation or activity that elevates one's energy level.

Energy Leak: a slow drainage of energy, sometimes barely noticeable.

Energy Sapper: a person, situation, or activity that drains one's energy level.

Stress: essentially, the rate of wear and tear on the body.

Stress Breaker: an activity that temporarily interrupts the state of being stressed.

Support Group/System: a network of people who assist each other by listening, problem solving or activities.

Syndrome: a combination of symptoms that usually occur together.

BIBLIOGRAPHY

1. Albrecht, E.: *Stress and the Manager.* Englewood Cliffs, Prentice-Hall, 1979.
2. Benson, H.: *The Relaxation Response.* New York, Avon, 1975.
3. Cherniss, G., Egnatios, E., and Wacher, S.: Job Stress and Career Development in New Public Professionals. *Professional Psychology,* November, 1976.
4. Freudenberger, H.: *The Staff Burnout Syndrome.* Washington, D.C., The Drug Abuse Council, Inc. (1828 I. St., N.W. 20036)
5. Kafry, D. and Pines, A.: *Coping Strategies and the Experience of Tedium.* Berkeley, University of California, 1978. Paper presented at American Psychological Convention, August, 1978.
6. Lamott, K.: *Escape from Stress.* New York, Berkeley Medallion, 1975.
7. Lazarus, R. and Cohen, J.: Environment Stress. *Human Behavior and Environment,* *1,* 1977.
8. Maslach, C. and Pines, A.: Burnout: The Loss of Human Caring. In *Experiencing Social Psychology.* Westminster, Maryland, Random House, in press.
9. Pearlin, L.I. and Schooler, C.: The Structure of Coping. *Journal of Health and Social Behavior, 10,* March, 1978.
10. Pines, A.: *How to Develop Detached Concern and Burnout.* Berkeley, University of California.
11. Selye, H.: *Stress Without Distress.* New York, Signet, 1974.
12. Selye, H.: *The Stress of Life.* New York, McGraw-Hill, 1956, updated, 1976.

Chapter 9

CHOOSING AN AIDE

Resource Specialist competencies covered in Chapter 9: The Resource Specialist must demonstrate the ability to—
1. define the job description of an instructional aide;
2. list the desired qualities in an aide;
3. clarify expectations of an aide;
4. supervise another person;
5. objectively evaluate the performance of the aide.

QUALITIES TO LOOK FOR IN AN AIDE

There has arisen many times in our careers as Resource Specialists, the concern that in all our many classes preparing us for this position, not a single one dealt with the problem of choosing an aide. This may not seem to be a critical point, but the aide plays an important part in the success of the program. As new Resource Specialists, we were not only confronted with setting up a program from scratch but also with the task of choosing an aide. We had to pull ourselves up out of the chaos of the new program long enough to choose an aide, tell her what we expected from her (we did not even know what we expected of ourselves yet) and proceed to direct this person. Everyone can relate to the experience with an aide that just did not work out quite well. Everyone can probably relate just as well to the time there was this aide who walked on water, the one who could run the program better than you could. After several years and numerous aides, we now know just exactly what to look for when choosing an aide.

The aide in the RSP room will assist the teacher in meeting the academic, physical, and at times the emotional needs of the student. The following qualifications have proven desirable:

1. generally neat appearance,
2. ability to adjust to a reasonable amount of flexibility in a changing program,

70

3. emotionally stable and mature,
4. ability to take direction and constructive criticism,
5. possess basic academic skills,
6. general understanding of handicapping conditions and knowledge of the types of students they will encounter,
7. prompt, responsible,
8. ability to set limits with students, enforce discipline and be consistent.

Good grooming is important when applying for any job. The aide must remember that he serves as a model for the students and should therefore present himself appropriately. This also serves as a reminder to the students that good grooming is an asset when looking for a job.

As mentioned before, the RSP program brings with it a great amount of change and the demand to be flexible. Daily lesson plans change as the needs of the students change, and the aide must be able to deal with this aspect of the program.

Students in RSP are there because they are experiencing some problems at school. Often these stem from problems in the home or other social areas. Any person attempting to deal with these students and their problems should be emotionally stable himself. It is very difficult to deal with the problems of others if you are experiencing your own. This is of no help to the students and certainly does not help your state of mind.

At all times the aide is under the general supervision of the RSP teacher. The teacher is responsible for the actions of the aide. For this reason the teacher wants to make certain that the aide fully understands his duties and is able to accept constructive criticism should the need arise. The ideal relationship between RSP teacher and aide is a complementary one. Most teachers do not like to order their aides around like children. A successful relationship will develop if each is aware of the other person's expectations and is willing to make his or her own needs known. The teacher should not expect the aide to know to help a student with a certain assignment if the aide has not been told of the importance of that. Likewise, the aide has the responsibility to inform the teacher if the teacher is not being clear as to what the expectations of the aide are.

A basic requirement for all aides is knowledge in the basic skill areas. Much of the curriculum that the aide will encounter at the high school level may be considered beyond the basic skill level, but this material can easily be learned. The most important thing to remember is where to find the answer if it is not known. We can all probably remember a time when a student came in with a math problem that presented a problem to us as well. "I knew that in high school and I just can't remember how to do it" is heard more often than you think, even in a Special Education classroom. The key to solving the problem is knowing where to look to help you solve the problem. This will be an important fact to pass on to the students. Many RSP students have problems retaining information, but their frustration will be lessened if they can just remember where to look for help.

It is only fair that the aide be informed about the students in the RSP classroom. Knowing what to expect will lessen anxiety about working with these students, increase awareness about handicaps, and aid in job performance. It is important that the aide be understanding yet not permissive. The aide will learn more about the students' strengths and weaknesses as the year goes on. Many districts offer in-service training for this. The aide should be encouraged to attend.

An aide must be responsible. No teacher, especially one as busy as an RSP teacher, needs to worry about an aide that is irresponsible. The teacher should come to feel confident with the aide and not be afraid to delegate tasks to the aide. The RSP teacher's duties may carry her outside the classroom often, and the teacher should not be reluctant to leave the students with the aide. Having an aide that you cannot depend on in this way will only hinder the program and not enable you to carry out your responsibilities.

Finally, an aide must be able to set behavior limits for the students and follow through with discipline procedures if necessary. The aide must be aware of the standards that the RSP teacher has set for the class and be willing to enforce these standards. Ideally, the aide will have the same basic philosophy regarding discipline that the teacher has, but this is not always possible. In that event, the aide must be willing to enforce the teachers' policies, provided they are reasonable. Consistency is the key to discipline for the aide as well as the teacher. The aide should know how to set limits, inform students of the logical consequences for noncompliance, and follow through. The teacher is responsible for making sure that the students realize they are to respect the aide just as they do the teacher and that they are to obey the aide at all times. Discipline will be maintained if the students are aware that the teacher and aide are working together and that they cannot get away with anything with either one.

RESPONSIBILITIES OF THE AIDE

The RSP aide has many different responsibilities. They may be categorized according to clerical duties, pupil assistance and teacher assistance.

Many RSP teachers choose to have their aides do only clerical tasks, while other teachers have their aides do none of this. It is definitely up to the teacher as to the amount of clerical work the aide performs. The following are some of the clerical duties the aide may perform:

1. prepare instructional materials,
2. duplicate materials,
3. keep daily records,
4. prepare progress reports to be sent to regular classroom teachers,
5. grade tests and correct papers,
6. maintain student folders.

Most RSP teachers choose to have their aides work with the students in the classroom. Most RSP classrooms find several different projects or assignments going on all at once. It seems that no two students are ever working on the same assignment. The aide can be a valuable asset in a situation like this. The following are some of the duties of the aide regarding pupil assistance:

1. assist with group or individual activities,
2. supervise children going to and from the RSP room,
3. assist in reading groups,
4. assist in giving tests for regular classroom teachers,
5. tutor individual students,
6. encourage students and give positive reinforcement,
7. brief students on missed or misunderstood assignments,
8. help students develop positive attitudes of self-worth,
9. monitor students working individually,
10. assist children with games.

There are a multitude of miscellaneous tasks that the aide may also be asked to do on occasion. These are all of valuable help to the RSP teacher. Some of these duties are as follows:

1. operate audio-visual equipment,
2. make telephone calls,
3. assist a regular teacher with RSP students,
4. give instruction to new aides or student aides,

5. assist in the preparation of lesson plans,
6. assist with assessment,
7. assist in detecting any health or behavioral problems,
8. accompany the class on field trips,
9. assist children to and from the bus or playground area.

In whatever manner the RSP teacher decides to use the aide, it is important to communicate needs, desires and feelings. Ideally, there should be a small part of each day set aside for the aide and teacher to sit down and plan together what the aide is to do. This is not always possible, and alternatives are required.

It may be possible to keep a notebook for the aide. In it could be recorded things the teacher would like the aide to do each day. This is a good way to maintain communication. It is very easy to forget to tell the aide something or thank him for doing something special. The teacher could make this part of her daily planning and thereby keep the aide informed and up to date on all aspects of the program. Some districts give RSP teachers one planning day each week. This gives the teacher and aide ample time to sit down together and plan for the coming week and evaluate the previous week's activities. This, too, is an ideal situation but does exist in some areas.

Now that some desired qualities of an aide and the responsibilities of the aide have been discussed, it is time to turn to the important task of actually choosing the right applicant. This is a very difficult task as some very capable aides may not interview well, and others may look terrific on paper but are not as competent in the classroom when it comes to working with the students. Besides this, when does the RSP teacher find the time to interview people applying for the position? Many districts take care of this part of the process, but many leave the final selection up to the RSP teacher. There are no clear-cut ways to insure that the best applicant will be selected, but there are systematic ways to narrow down the choice.

There are several points that should not go unmentioned in the interview with each prospective aide:

1. job description,
2. expectations of the RSP teacher,
3. job responsibilities,
4. previous experiences of the applicant,

5. brief knowledge of handicaps (particularly learning handicaps) on the part of the applicant,
6. brief statement of the applicant's philosophy regarding the role of the aide in the Special Education classroom.

The interviewer may also want to make a rating scale on each applicant, including scores from general appearance to knowledge of basic skills. Immediate response to these criteria will later aid the interviewer in the final selection. It is always impossible to know for sure if a person will prove to be successful on the basis of an interview alone. The applicants may want to see the room in which they may be working. Some may even offer to come in for a short period of time to work and see if they would really like the job. Choosing the aide may be perhaps the most difficult aspect of working with the aide. No one wants to go through all the time involved in interviewing only to find three months later that the person just is not suited for the position, as the following case illustrates.

> Joan was a bright girl of twenty-three. She had a great personality and was very neatly groomed. It seemed during the interview that she would be an asset to any classroom. She had a good knowledge of high school curriculum, had been a playground leader, and was working on a teaching credential. The RSP teacher was very pleased with Joan during the interview and hired her on the spot. Everything went fine for the first few weeks. Joan proved to be a hard worker. She liked the students, and they all liked her. She liked her job very much. The teacher did not leave Joan alone in the classroom these first few weeks. As Joan became more confident of herself in her new surroundings, the teacher decided that she could once again resume some of her other responsibilities that at times took her out of the classroom. She explained to Joan what she wanted her to do with the students in her absence, and left to go meet with a counselor. The teacher returned to find the room a mess. Students were sitting on top of the desks, which was not allowed when the teacher was around. Other students had turned on a radio and were beginning to dance over in one corner. A fight had just begun in the back office, and there stood Joan, not at all annoyed with the activities in the room. After a couple of phone calls home, a referral to the office, and confiscation of the radio until a later date, the teacher overlooked Joan's inability to handle the situation this time because she had been so pleased with the rest

of Joan's performance. She assured Joan that she did not approve of this type of behavior but offered no suggestions as to how Joan should have handled the situation. After this episode, the teacher always stepped in when inappropriate behavior presented itself. She came to Joan's rescue and asserted her own authority. This, too, finally got out of hand. Each time the teacher left the classroom, she would return to find a worse situation than the last time. The teacher finally sat down with Joan to try to resolve the problem. The teacher admitted that she found it easier to step in and handle matters and felt justified in doing so because Joan was so competent in other areas. These are the things they both agreed upon:

1. The teacher emphasized her classroom policies and consequences for noncompliance. Joan agreed to abide by these and enforce them as the teacher would.
2. The teacher would tell the students that she expected them to behave appropriately when she was in the room and when she left them with the aide. She stated that the consequences would be the same if they acted inappropriately for the aide just as they were if they did so for her.
3. The teacher agreed to review various behavior management techniques with the aide. Joan even thought that she would look into taking a Behavior Management course at school.
4. Until both the teacher and Joan were assured that the activities of the past would not repeat themselves each time the teacher left the room, the teacher agreed to leave the room only in an emergency.

All of these steps were tried but did not remedy the situation. Joan, being very small and soft spoken, could not assert herself with the students. She felt that it was important to always give the student another chance. This was something the teacher did not favor. Joan tried, but her basic philosophy of discipline was so different from that of the teacher. The inconsistency was not good for the students or for Joan and the teacher. Despite her competence in other areas, Joan just could not be left alone with the students any longer. The teacher now had to make a very critical decision whether to keep Joan and put up with the problem or try to find another aide in the middle of the school year.

This entire conflict could have been resolved if proper screening had taken place before Joan started to work. The teacher did not have the time to interview other applicants; Joan seemed bright, likeable, and willing to work hard, so she was hired on the spot. However, the teacher never mentioned discipline during the interview. If she had, she would have found that Joan did not believe in a lot of structure and was not a strict disciplinarian. She did, in fact, have many excellent qualities but none as critical as a strong behavior management philosophy. Her other assets did not prove to be all that valuable because she had no sense of discipline. This is a key issue in Special Education and should not be passed over in an interview. The teacher should keep these points in mind when interviewing applicants as it could present future conflicts.

Chapter 10

NO TIME FOR CAREER EDUCATION

Resource Specialist competencies covered in Chapter 10: The Resource Specialist must demonstrate the ability to:
1. develop resources and activities related to the three levels of career development;
2. differentiate between vocational and career education;
3. develop vocational goals for IEPs appropriate to the student's needs.

The emphasis on mainstreaming and teaching survival skills has made it difficult for RSP teachers to set aside the time to teach occupational preparation. Many RSP teachers have expressed their frustration over not enough time to teach career education. RSP teachers have tried to compensate for this by working with content area teachers to infuse appropriate career experiences into the curriculum. There are questions the RSP teacher will need to answer as to whether this instruction is enough to make the RSP student occupationally ready for the world of work. For some RSP students the exposure in the regular classroom will be enough; others will need more concentrated instruction in the RSP room. On the secondary level the RSP teacher will constantly be faced with the low achieving student who has had years of remediation. The decision must be made whether to continue with remediation or set up a program that would provide the student with the necessary skills for job readiness. This is, of course, the decision of the IEP team.

In this chapter references have been made to career education and vocational education. Although both terms deal with the world of work, they are not synonymous.

> Career education is designed for all students from kindergarten through adulthood. It takes place in instructional programs at all levels of education, which can be taught by all instructors. Career education is based on teaching students the many skills they will need to satisfy the different roles in their life.

Vocational education involves job entry training which usually takes place on the secondary level. It is a general course taught by instructors trained in vocational areas which focus on paid employment. (Brolin & Kokaska 1979)

Career education occurs throughout an individual's lifetime; however, a student's exposure to career education is broken into three stages of development: (1) career awareness, (2) career exploration, and (3) career preparation. At the elementary level, career awareness is the primary focus. While the emphasis is mainly at the elementary level, career awareness does surface continually throughout the individual's life. Attitude, information, and self-awareness are three major elements of career awareness. Work values are very important concepts, and an introduction to positive work values at an early age will certainly lay a sound foundation for positive attitudes in the future. Much of the teaching of career awareness can be done easily through career infusion in the regular classroom by scheduling guest speakers, field trips, and classroom career awareness activities. Listed at the end of this chapter are activities that may be infused into the regular classroom curriculum. Career infusion may not always take place in the regular classroom, especially in the upper grade content areas. If appropriate instruction is not taking place, the RSP teacher may want to supply the instruction in the RSP room.

Career exploration has its primary emphasis during the junior high or middle school years. During this phase the student carefully examines his talents, abilities and needs. The student continues to explore work and personal values as they relate to careers with the addition of hands-on experiences through prevocational classes such as industrial arts and home economics. During this phase the student begins to explore more realistic career goals. Students may begin taking on part-time jobs such as baby-sitting, gardening and paper deliveries. These experiences provide the teacher with an excellent opportunity to bring actual student work experiences into the classroom. The RSP teacher may want to work with school personnel to set up work exploration sites on the school campus for older RSP students who are ready for this experience. Though this may involve a lot of extra work for the RSP teacher, the rewards reaped by the students are invaluable. At this age students are more willing to work for the job experience rather than money. There are many advantages to this. It helps the student make an easier transition when ready for paid employment out in the community. The student also works in a semi-sheltered environment with school personnel aware of the RSP teacher's goals for the students, enabling the RSP teacher to handle problem situations more easily as soon as they arise.

It is very important for the RSP teacher to keep in close contact with the prevocational teachers to insure success for the RSP students in their classes. Many RSP students transfer to a secondary school without the experience of prevocational classes. One of the main reasons for this is that they were transfered out of the class because the teacher was either not aware of, or did not know how to deal with, some of the problems that student was having in class. Many of these situations can be avoided if there is a closer working relationship with prevocational teachers. The RSP student with no prevocational experience is at a disadvantage at the high school level. He is not only competing with other students who may have had prevocational experiences, but many RSP students often require a longer period of time to develop skills in certain areas. It should be remembered when working with these teachers that they have valuable expertise in their field and are probably not aware of the impact they have on RSP students. These teachers are valuable people who can assist in meeting the needs of RSP students.

Along with the other phases of career development, career preparation is not solely confined to one period of the student's schooling. The main emphasis of development occurs at the high school level. At this stage, most RSP students require a heavy experiential component. The use of the Work Experience coordinator becomes extremely important at this phase. The student may begin his experience with an on-campus job or, if he has already had this experience, he may be ready for an off-campus job experience. Job placement should be carefully supervised. A student should not be sent out for a job interview unless he is job-ready.

Although each phase of career development is presented at different grade levels, students do not always progress at the same stage. One student may be ready for career exploration at the junior high level, while another student may not be ready for this phase until high school.

With the passage of Senate Bill 1870, many districts or consortiums have attempted to address the vocational component in the law by hiring vocational program specialists or vocational counselors in the area of Special Education to assist the RSP teacher with vocational planning for students. As stated previously, it is up to the IEP team to decide what type of plan is more appropriate for the individual student. However, for many RSP students who are having problems succeeding in school, the only relevant subject matter for them may be that which directly relates to getting a job after school.

On the secondary level, career education may be sufficiently infused into content areas to meet the needs of many RSP students. Two approaches may be used in meeting these needs. One approach would be to meet with the content area teacher to see how you could assist with curriculum modification and how receptive the teacher may be to career education infusion. Many RSP teachers are taking another approach by developing a career education course within the RSP program. This may be on an awareness and/or exploration level. Grants may be written to assist the RSP teacher in creating programs that would meet the needs of students. There are many other types of grants also available for this purpose.

Vocational classes that are meeting the needs of RSP students are being established in high schools across the country. With the advent of P.L. 94-142, P.L. 93-112, and P.L. 93-142, it is mandated that appropriate occupational preparation take place within the handicapped student's school program. This requires extensive consultation and planning with vocational educators and program specialists. This has already brought about many changes in curriculum adjustment and teaching styles and is proving itself to be of benefit to the students by providing them with improved vocational services. We still have a lot of work ahead if we are to continue to upgrade the employability of handicapped individuals.

CAREER INTEREST ASSESSMENT

The assessment of a student's interest and abilities can serve many useful purposes. Many students are uncertain about what they want to do when they finish school, and they also wonder at what they would be successful. Disabled youth desperately need objective information about their strengths and weaknesses and how these aptitudes match up to their career interests. Many of their questions can be answered by vocational assessment.

Vocational assessment is most often used to help select a specific vocational program for a student. It is important to be cautious in interpreting the test results. A prediction of future success in a given vocational area interpreted by test results does not necessarily mean that the students will be guaranteed success on a job in the related area. There are many other factors that must be considered in matching potential jobs with students. Aptitude testing can only give the teacher certain indicators for student abilities that may be applied to a specific vocational area.

Career interest testing suggests certain career cluster areas a student might be interested in based on test results.

APTITUDE ASSESSMENT

Aptitude tests (work samples) are usually real or simulated work tasks administered to assess various traits or characteristics of students. These characteristics usually include behavior, aptitude and attitude.

There are many types of paper-and-pencil aptitude tests available. Many RSP students do not do as well on this type of testing because of their disabilities with reading and writing. Commercially produced simulated work tasks are very expensive, but they are becoming more prevalent for use with handicapped individuals. The need for appropriate aptitude assessment is now being addressed at all levels by educational institutions. Grants are being written to help establish vocational assessment centers in school districts. One common source of funding has been the vocational discretionary funds under P.L. 94-142.

Many of the career assessment centers that have been developed in school districts or different organizations use a number of different assessments. Care must be taken to evaluate thoroughly each assessment to insure that it properly meets the needs of the students. One assessment tool will rarely be enough; the RSP teacher should develop a battery that can be used for many students.

VOCATIONAL COMPONENT IN THE IEP

New state and federal laws have substantially changed the requirement for providing vocational education for Special Education students. Under these laws, educational institutions must insure that a disabled student's vocational skills and needs are appropriately assessed and that vocational services are tailored to individuals' needs and provided in a nondiscriminatory manner.

The primary requirement of P.L. 94-142 and S.B. 1870 is the development of an Individualized Educational Program for each student. Under these laws, vocational education programs are to be included in the IEP on the transition plan.

The phrase "when appropriate" is up to the interpretation of the educational institution. Some districts have interpreted "when appropriate" to mean a vocational goal must be written for every student in Special Education from seventh to twelfth grade. Other school districts have interpreted the law to cover those students from grade seven to twelve who are not receiving appropriate vocational experiences in regular classes. This may be covered in a vocational class or through career experience in the regular classroom. If modification has taken place to fit the student's needs, a goal must be included in the IEP. Ultimately, it is the responsibility of the RSP teacher to monitor the vocational component of the IEP.

MODIFYING TEACHING STYLE
AND VOCATIONAL CURRICULUM

1. Supply the vocational teachers with the reading levels of all RSP students.
2. Help vocational teachers determine reading levels of all printed materials.
3. Assist vocational teachers in the selection of materials that are appropriate for students' abilities.
4. Provide clear and complete directions for each assignment. This may be given orally and visually (written on the board or handout). Let the student know what is to be learned from the assignment.
5. Shortened assignments may be used as an alternative for students with reading problems.
6. Teach vocabulary critical for understanding concepts. Do not assume that the student understands the terms presented.
7. Preteach selected key words.
8. Preteach the multiple meanings of vocational terms. Do not assume that the student can make inference regarding this.
9. Use concrete demonstrations generously.
10. Provide lots of practice, but avoid meaningless repetition.
11. Evaluate frequently and reassure students to compensate for past failures and frustrations.
12. Provide for progress checks so students are able to monitor their progress.
13. Assist students in the development of their vocational ambitions. They should be realistically founded.

14. Develop materials when necessary that are appropriate to the students' needs.
    a. Place materials on audio-tape.
    b. Use photos on a display board to help show the sequence of specific procedures.
    c. Develop slide/tape materials to teach concepts and/or procedures.
    d. Highlight important phrases and terms on printed material.
    e. Place technical vocabulary on language cards so that students may have the combination audio/visual presentation.
15. Handouts, learning packets, and tests should be simplified.
    a. Avoid long, complex sentences.
    b. Use punctuation sparingly.
    c. Avoid irrelevant words, phrases and sentences.
    d. Avoid multisyllabic words whenever possible.
    e. Use illustrations that do not distract students.
    f. Give few and simple directions.
16. Consider alternative grading systems.
    a. student contracts
    b. competence based
    c. "limited" certificates
    Be sure to list explicitly what the student can and cannot do when developing these systems of grading for prospective employers.
17. Use technical or peer tutors whenever possible.

BIBLIOGRAPHY

1. Bhaerman, R.O.: The ERIC Clearinghouse on Adult, Career, and Vocational Education, National Center for Research in Vocational Education, 1979.
2. Brock, R.J.: *Preparing Vocational and Special Education Personnel to Work with Special Needs Students.* State of the Art, 1977, University of Wisconsin, 1977.
3. Brolin, I.E. and Kokaska, C.J.: *Career Education for Handicapped Children and Youth.* Columbus, Ohio, Merrill, 1979.
4. Ecksten, B.J.: Research Grant Studies. New York, 1980–1981.
5. Gronlund, N.E.: *Stating Behavioral Objectives for Classroom Instruction.* New York, Macmillan, 1970.
6. Phelps, L.A. and Lutz, R.J.: *Career Exploration and Preparation for the Special Needs Learner.* Boston, Allyn & Bacon, 1977.
7. Torres, S.: *A Primer on Individualized Education Programs for Handicapped Children.* Reston, Virginia, The Foundation for Exceptional Children, 1977.

8. ERIC Clearinghouse on Career Education, The Center for Vocational Education, The Ohio State University, 1960, Kenny Road, Columbus, Ohio 43210.

9. ERIC Clearinghouse on Handicapped and Gifted Children. The Council for Exceptional Children, 1920 Association Drive, Reston, Virginia 22091.

10. National Information Center for Special Education Materials (NIMIS II). University of Southern California, University Park, Los Angeles, California 90007.

11. National Center for Career Education. P.O. Box 7815, Missoula, Montana 59801.

12. Regional Resources Center/Specialized Offices. California Regional Resources Center, 1031 S. Broadway, Suite 623, Los Angeles, California 90007.

TABLE IV

ACTIVITIES FOR CAREER EDUCATION

Level	Activity	Materials	Related Academic Areas						
			Reading	Lang. Arts	Math	Soc. Studies	Health/Sci.	Art/Music	Home Ec.
Gr. k - 3 Awareness	Make a collage of pictures showing different family activities and chores. Discuss each one and how each family member cooperates to get all the household work done.	magazines scissors glue or paste		X		X	X	X	
	Discuss which community workers could help if you get lost or need help at home. Discuss safety factors. Help each student make a list of emergency phone numbers to post at home.	paper pencil		X		X	X		
	Have students pantomime workers doing various jobs while other students guess what job they are doing.			X					
	Bring a variety of hats representing different jobs (nurse's cap, fireman's hat, hard hat). Have students name the job that goes with each. Then write the job on a flash card and have students match cards with each hat. Have student try on hats and pretend to do the job of the person who wears that hat.	pencil or marking pens flash cards hats	X	X		X			

Level	Activity	Materials	Related Academic Areas						
			Reading	Lang. Arts	Math	Soc.Studies	Health/Sci.	Art/Music	Home Ec.
	Play a game matching tools or pictures of tools to pictures of workers. Graduate to matching to simple flash cards with jobs written on them.	tools magazines flashcards pencil or marking pen	X	X		X			
	Invite the school custodian to visit class to discuss his duties. Ask him to bring samples of the tools he uses and explain briefly how he uses each.	custodian materials used by custodian		X			X		
	Visit various school workers and have students list the duties of each. Plan ahead what questions the students will ask of the workers.	paper pencil school workers		X		X			
	Have students list as many different workers as they can that they see on their way to school each day.	paper pencil		X		X			
	Invite workers from different areas to class to talk about their jobs. Have them bring sample tools or materials that they use to show to the children. Whenever possible, visit local grocery and department stores, restaurants, fire and police departments to see these workers in action on their job sites.								

Level	Activity	Materials	Reading	Lang. Arts	Math	Soc.Studies	Health/Sci.	Art/Music	Home Ec.
	Play Bingo matching pictures to simple vocabulary words that the students have learned (the teacher would say firefighter and the students may have a picture of a fire truck or fire hydrant).	Bingo cards with pictures playing pieces for use as Bingo chips	X	X					
	Take pictures of workers on field trips and use them as a follow-up activity to have students write a short story about each picture.	camera paper pencil		X		X			
	Conduct a treasure hunt to locate career related items. Place a number of carpenter tools around the room, for example, and have the students locate them. Then ask each child to tell the class what each tool is used for. Discretion should be used so as not to use dangerous tools or instruments.	tools		X					
	Take a walk through the school neighborhood and look for different signs. At school find these signs in magazines or make large pictures of them to hang around the room. Discuss what each means.	poster board paints or marking pens		X			X	X	

Column header group: Related Academic Areas

Level	Activity	Materials	Related Academic Areas						
			Reading	Lang. Arts	Math	Soc. Studies	Health/Sci.	Art/Music	Home Ec.
	Visit a home construction site and discuss safety rules. Have students look for ways in which physical skills are used, math skills and reading skills. How many different types of workers were there at the site?			X		X	X		
Gr. 4 - 6 Orientation	On a 3 x 5 card have each student write one of his/her parents' occupations. Help the student with the spelling. Put the cards in a box, mix them up, and have students take turns pulling out a card and describing the job they selected.	3 x 5 cards pencil empty box	X	X		X			
	Invite high school students who work at local job sites (gas stations, fast-food chains, grocery stores) to speak to class about their jobs and what skills learned in school are necessary for those jobs.								
	Cut out newspaper ads and coupons for a classroom grocery store. Use these for math problems for such things as making change, adding, simple planning and budgeting.	newspaper scissors pencils paper	X	X	X				

Level	Activity	Materials	Reading	Lang. Arts	Math	Soc. Studies	Health/Sci.	Art/Music	Home Ec.
	Using the above, give students $5.00 and have them plan a picnic.		X		X				
	Keep a row of boxes on a counter for drug store items, grocery store items, hardware store items, etc. Cut out pictures of these items and place in appropriate box. Have students shop for these items and make change from play money bills.	empty boxes magazines scissors play money paper pencil	X	X	X	X		X	
	Obtain brochures and maps from a travel agency and have students plan an imaginary trip.	brochures maps paper pens, pencils							
	Bake bread or cookies in class. Write each step of the recipe down in order for each student to have a copy.	Cooking utensils ingredients paper pencil	X	X	X				
	Have a bake sale and have students record all earnings and expenses. Plan how profits are to be used - field trip, class party.	baked goods paper pencil poster board	X	X	X	X			

Related Academic Areas

Level	Activity	Materials	Reading	Lang. Arts	Math	Soc.Studies	Health/Sci.	Art/Music	Home Ec.
	Have students list all community workers they come into contact with each week. Compare lists and discuss the duties of each.	paper pencil	X	X		X	X		
	Arrange for students to take on simple jobs around the classroom or school for one week, (cafeteria, with custodian, office, playground) and have each report on their duties and skills required.	paper pencil	X	X		X	X		
	Play the alphabet career game. Begin with the letter "a" by naming a job starting with that letter and so on.			X					
	Give students worksheets with a list of categories such as plumbing, new car dealers, shoe repair, etc. Using the Yellow Pages, have students look up at least three places that fit in each category. Students may be paired up to work in groups.	Yellow Pages paper pencil	X	X					
	Have students categorize jobs into three areas: (1) working with your hands, (2) working with numbers and (3) working with people. Have them pick their area of preference.	paper pencil	X	X		X			

Level	Activity	Materials	Reading	Lang. Arts	Math	Soc.Studies	Health/Sci.	Art/Music	Home Ec.
	Include a Career Column in each issue of your school newspaper. Students take turns reporting on different jobs, interviewing workers, and reporting their findings. You may wish to compile a basic interview format for each interview.	paper pencil school paper	X	X		X		X	
Gr. 7 - 9 Exploration	Have students list their hobbies and interests in two columns -- free activities and those requiring a charge. List any possible career choices that relate to any of these.	paper pen/pencil			X				

	Look up and record on 5 x 8 cards local service numbers for use at home.
	  police
	  fire department
	  ambulance
	  paramedic
	  emergency hospital
	  doctor
	  parents work phone
	  school
	  neighbor
		5 x 8 index cards
		pen/pencil
						X	X		

Level	Activity	Materials	Reading	Lang. Arts	Math	Soc.Studies	Health/Sci.	Art/Music	Home Ec.
	Have students keep a journal of job listings. When they encounter someone with a different job, list it with any information they can find out about the job (training required, necessary skills, etc.)	paper or notebook pen/pencil				X			
	Have each student prepare a daily schedule of their own activities. School, homework, and household chores should be included as well as free time.	paper or notebook pen/pencil							
	Write paragraphs following district format on various jobs and their opportunities.	paper pen/pencil		X		X			
	Create a mobile for the classroom or for students' rooms. Mobile may include pictures of tools used on various jobs and various pictured aspects of different jobs.	scissors string glue magazines				X		X	
	Have students prepare a report on the costs of owning an automobile other than the actual cost of the car. Include: gas oil tune-ups other upkeep insurance license registration	paper pen/pencil			X				

Level	Activity	Materials	Reading	Lang. Arts	Math	Soc.Studies	Health/Sci.	Art/Music	Home Ec.
	Discuss taxes and what things are paid for by taxes. Make a collage of things paid for by taxes. Or make a mobile of the same.	scissors glue magazines string poster board						X	
	Using department store catalogs, have students buy Christmas gifts for their families on a $100.00 budget.	paper pen/pencil store catalogs			X				
	Using department store catalogs, have students buy back-to-school clothes on a $200.00 budget. Don't forget shoes, underwear, and a new winter coat; not just jeans and tops.	paper pen/pencil store catalogs			X				
	Create a product! In addition to the design include package plans advertising plans accounting cost of production investment plans for your profit	paper pen/pencil drawing paper ruler paints or marking pens			X			X	

Level	Activity	Materials	Reading	Lang. Arts	Math	Soc.Studies	Health/Sci.	Art/Music	Home Ec.
	Invite workers and/or supervisors of various jobs to class to discuss the training and skills necessary for their jobs. Have each interview one student for that job while other students take notes for later discussion. Good sources are local fast-food restaurants, grocery stores, and department stores.								
	Invite a representative for the State Employment Office to visit class and discuss job opportunities for the future.				X	X			
	Visit a computer center.				X				
	Discuss grooming and dress as they relate to different jobs. Role-play correct and incorrect ways to dress for different jobs.					X			X
	Collect sample job applications from local sources. Go over them with the class and compare and contrast them. List items that are common to all applications.	paper pen/pencil			X	X			
	Have students list the qualities of a good supervisor. Role-play job situations depicting "good" and "bad" supervisors.	paper pen/pencil				X			

Level	Activity	Materials	Related Academic Areas						
			Reading	Lang. Arts	Math	Soc.Studies	Health/Sci.	Art/Music	Home Ec.
Gr. 9 - 12 Preparation Level	Discuss attributes that would increase job success.					X			
	Have students list their own positive and negative traits.	paper pen				X	X		
	Go on field trips to different job sites.					X			
	Have students interview someone from the business or industrial world. Discuss interview questions and format before beginning.	paper pen				X			
	Role-play a number of different job situations in which the employee and the employer are showing different types of emotions, and discuss how the situations should be handled.					X	X		
	Discuss emotions -- shy, hostile, angry, afraid, hurt. Discuss how a person may behave on the job when feeling these different emotions.					X	X		

Level	Activity	Materials	Reading	Lang. Arts	Math	Soc.Studies	Health/Sci.	Art/Music	Home Ec.
	Have students think of a time in their lives when they have felt each of these emotions. Have each relate an incident and how he behaved. Have each evaluate whether the behavior was appropriate or inappropriate.			X		X	X		
	Role-play different job situations which exhibit appropriate and inappropriate reactions to events taking place. The teacher will have to create most of the situations and write them on cards for the students to act out.					X			
	Have students answer a brief questionnaire about themselves. From this, have them write an auto-biography.	paper pen		X					
	Discuss criteria required for an interview. Develop good questions for the interview and then stage interviews for specific jobs (found possibly in the want ads). Videotape each interview if possible and discuss each one with the class.	video equipment				X			

MATERIALS RESOURCE

P - Primary   I - Intermediate   S - Secondary   A - Adult

Reading/Language Arts	Skill Level	Interest Level	Publisher
Bestellers	P	I, S	Fearon, Janus, Quercus
Clues For Better Reading	P, I	P, I	Curriculum Associates
Clues For Better Writing	P	P, I	Curriculum Associates
English For Everyday Living	P	I, S	Ideal
Fearon High Interest, Low Level Readers	P	I, S	Fearon, Janus, Quercus
Instant Spelling	P-A	P-A	Curriculum Associates
Learning Through Literature	P	I, S	Curriculum Associates
Life Skills English	P	I, S	AGS
Pacemaker Classics/True Adventure Series	P	I, S	Fearon, Janus, Quercus
Peer Voices	P	I, S	Curriculum Associates
Readability Rater	P-A	P-A	Academic Therapy
Recording For The Blind 215 East 58th Street New York, NY 10022			
Sight Word Lab	P	I, S	DLM
Silly Sounds Games	P	P	Ideal
Skills For Success	P-S	P-S	Curriculum Associates
Spector Suspense Series	P	I, S	Fearon, Janus, Quercus
Spellex Word Finder	P-A	P-A	Curriculum Associates
Sportellers Series	P	I, S	Fearon, Janus, Quercus
Thirty Lessons In Outlining	P	I, S	Curriculum Associates

P - Primary   I - Intermediate   S - Secondary   A - Adult

Math	Skill Level	Interest Level	Publisher
"21"	P	All	Any deck of cards
Flash Cards	P	P- S	Kenworthy Ed. Services
Math in Action	P, I	I, S	Fearon, Janus, Quercus
Pacemaker Practical Arithmetic Series	P	P-S	Fearon, Janus, Quercus

Content Areas			
Fearon's Pacemaker Curriculum 　General Science Series 　Life, Earth & Physical Science 　　Series 　Science In Action Series	P	I-A	Fearon, Janus, Quercus
Fearon Pacemaker Curriculum 　Economics Course 　Geography Skills 　Government and Civics 　Nation Builders Biographies 　United States History 　World History Makers	P	I-S	Fearon, Janus, Quercus

Study Skills			
Pre-Referral Intervention Manual	P-S	P-S	Hawthorne Ed. Services
Skills For School Success	P-S	I, S	Curriculum Associates
Thirty Lessons In Outlining	P	I, S	Curriculum Associates
WGC-R Compilation What To Do Now That You Know 　the Score	P-S	P-S	Academic Therapy

P - Primary   I - Intermediate   S - Secondary   A - Adult

Vocational	Skill Level	Interest Level	Publisher
Job Application File	P, I	S	Fearon, Janus, Quercus
Job Box	P, I	S	Fearon, Janus, Quercus
Job Interview Guide	P, I	S	Fearon, Janus, Quercus
Job Planner	P, I	S	Fearon, Janus, Quercus
Pacemaker Vocational Readers	P, I	S	Fearon, Janus, Quercus
Seven Keys to Work Success	P	S	Fearon, Janus, Quercus

A.D.D. Warehouse
300 Northwest 70th Avenue
Plantation, Florida 33317
1 (305) 792-8944

AGS
American Guidance Service
4201 Woodland Road
P.O. Box 99
Circle Pines, Minnesota 55014
1 (800) 328-2560

Academic Therapy Publications
20 Commercial Boulevard
Novato, California 94947
1 (415) 883-3314

Catalog of Instructional Tapes for
  Handicapped Students
  (preschool - University)
Clearinghouse Depositor for
  Handicapped Students
California State Department of
  Education
Tape Duplicating Center/CDHS
721 Capitol Mall
Sacramento, California 95814
1 (916) 445-1290

Curriculum Assoc., Inc.
5 Esquire Road
North Billerica, Massachusetts 018623
1-800-225-0248

Developmental Learning Material
P.O. Box 400
One DLM Park
Allen, Texas 75002
1 (800) 527-4747

EDSCO Curriculum Materials
Box 11542
Birmingham, Alabama 35202
1 (800) 633-8623

Fearon, Janus, Quercus
500 Harbor Boulevard
Belmont, California 94002
1 (800) 877-4283

Follett Publishing Co.
1010 West Washington
Chicago, Illinois

Frank Schaffer Publications, Inc.
26616 Indian Peak Road
Palos Verdes Peninsula, CA 90274

Hawthorne Educational Services
800 Gray Oak Drive
Columbia, Ohio 65201
1 (800) 542-1673

Lakeshore Curriculum Materials
2695 East Dominguez Street
P:. O. Box 6261
Carson, California 90749
1 (310) 537-8600

Modern Curriculum Press
13900 Prospect Road
Cleveland, Ohio 44136
1 (800) 321-3106

Pro Ed
8700 Shoal Creek Boulevard
Austin, Texas 78758
1 (512) 451-3246

Wieser Educational, Inc.
30085 Comercio
Rancho Santa Margarita, CA 92688
1 (714) 858-4920

INDEX